"This Is My Reservation, I Belong Here"

The Salish Kootenai Indian Struggle Against Termination

"This Is My Reservation, I Belong Here"

The Salish Kootenai Indian Struggle Against Termination

by
Jaakko Puisto

published by
Salish Kootenai College Press
Pablo, Montana

distributed by
University of Nebraska Press
Lincoln, Nebraska

2016

Front Cover illustrations: Top, Walter McDonald, source, Confederated Salish and Kootenai Tribes, Pablo, Montana. Bottom: Jerome Hewankorn and Montana congressional delegation, source: Mike Mansfield Papers MSS 065, photograph 99-2314, Archives and Special Collections, Mansfield Library, University of Montana, Missoula, Montana.

Back Cover Illustration: Senator James Murray, source: photograph 81-10, Archives and Special Collections, Mansfield Library, University of Montana, Missoula, Montana.

Library of Congress Cataloging-in-Publication Data:
Names: Puisto, Jaakko, author.
Title: "This is my reservation, I belong here": the Salish Kootenai Indian struggle against termination / by Jaakko Puisto.
Other titles: Salish Kootenai Indian struggle against termination
Description: Pablo, Montana: Salish Kootenai College Press distributed by University of Nebraska Press, Lincoln, Nebraska, [2016] | Includes bibliographical references and index.
Identifiers: LCCN 2016048507 | ISBN 9781934594186 (pbk.)
Subjects: LCSH: Salish Indians--History--20th century. | Kootenai Indians--History--20th century. | Flathead Indian Reservation (Mont.)--History--20th century. | Confederated Salish & Kootenai Tribes of the Flathead Reservation, Montana--History. | Salish Indians--Legal status, laws, etc.--Montana--Flathead Indian Reservation. | Kootenai Indians--Legal status, laws, etc.--Montana--Flathead Indian Reservation. | Salish Indians--Government relations. | Indian termination policy--Montana--Flathead Indian Reservation. | Self-determination, National--Montana--Flathead Indian Reservation.
Classification: LCC E99.S2 P85 2016 | DDC 978.6004/979435--dc23
LC record avilable at https://lccn.loc.gov/2016048507

Distributed by University of Nebraska Press, 1111 Lincoln Mall, Lincoln, NE 68588-0630, order 1-800-755-1105, www.nebraskapress.unl.edu.

Table of Contents

Preface

The Salish and Kootenai tribes first came into contact with the United States early in the nineteenth century when they met the Lewis and Clark Expedition. Soon the tribes had to fight for their homelands coveted by the same United States. This fight included signing a treaty with the U.S. in 1855, which limited their homelands significantly. However, the tribal leaders made the agreement to secure a military alliance with the United States against the Blackfeet, not to give up their lands. Later the U.S. Congress broke this treaty by legislating the allotment of the Salish and Kootenai lands in the early twentieth century. After moving back towards self-rule with the Indian Reorganization Act constitution in the 1930s, the tribes again had to defend their homelands against a congressional effort to terminate their reservation in the 1950s. This book focuses on this battle against termination. The Salish and Kootenai people themselves are in the center of the story.

It needs to be emphasized that only part of the story can be gathered from the historical record, such as *Congressional Record*, National Archives, and newspaper accounts. While some interviews have been utilized, there is a lot to be done to fill the gaps in the story. Ultimately only the Salish and Kootenai themselves can fully tell what happened during the termination debates. Also important is to note that the perception of the threat of termination did not go away with the congressional campaign of the 1950s, but extended into the beginning of the twenty-first century, as the last chapter of this book demonstrates.

Most of this book is a revised version of my 2000 PhD dissertation at Arizona State University, "'This is My Reservation,

I Belong Here': The Salish Kootenai Struggle Against Termination," University Microfilms International 9976334. The major part of chapter 4 is reprinted from the *American Indian Culture and Research Journal*, volume 33, number 2, pages 45-66, by permission of the American Indian Studies Center, University of California, Los Angeles, copyright 2016 Regents of the University of California.

The author wishes to thank the Salish and Kootenai people for their warm reception on the reservation. Special thanks go to the Salish and Pend d'Oreille Culture Committee of St. Ignatius and the Kootenai Culture Committee of Elmo, and all the elders I interviewed. I also want to thank Thompson Smith for help during the research process and Bob Bigart of Salish Kootenai College Press for getting this book into publication.

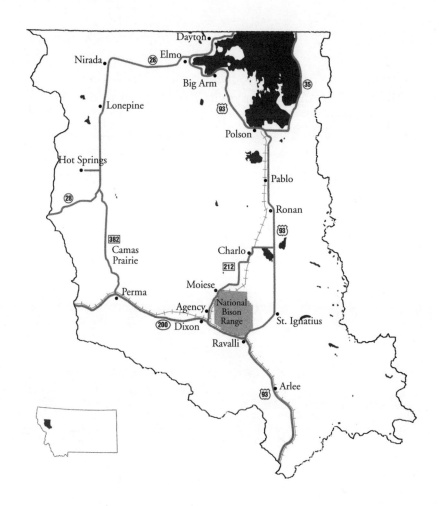

Flathead Indian Reservation, Montana

Map by Wyatt Design, Helena, Montana.

Chapter 1

Introduction

From the vantage point of busy Highway 93, the first sight of the Flathead Reservation does not suggest a homeland for tribal people. One has to be able to see signs such as the Flathead Trading Post and Museum in St. Ignatius or the tribal headquarters and college in Pablo, all just off the main highway, to recognize an Indian presence. After entering the reservation one first arrives at the Jocko River Valley and the community of Arlee, named after the former Salish chief. Another fifteen miles and a climb over some hills brings the visitor to the wide Flathead River Valley with the towering Mission Mountain Range to the east and the old mission in the center of the village of St. Ignatius. This is some of the most scenic country in the world. Another thirty miles to the north the glimmering waters of Flathead Lake, the largest fresh water pool in the entire state, greet the visitor. To the west lies the rugged canyon of the Flathead River and the Salish Mountains, which divide the reservation into two valleys. On the west side lies the Little Bitterroot River Valley before the outer reaches of the Cabinet Mountains bring one to the reservation boundary. At Flathead Lake lies the non-Indian community of Polson, but the reservation reaches north another twenty miles on both sides of the lake. This is home to some 20,000 people, 4,000 of them members of the Salish and Kootenai tribes. This is the reservation which Congress and the federal government wanted to terminate in the 1950s. When one visits this beautiful place, with its big sky of Montana legend, one can understand tribal opposition to this effort.

* * * * * * * *

The 1855 Hellgate Treaty

To understand the key arguments presented in the termination debate of the 1950s, it is essential to familiarize oneself with how the Flathead Indian Reservation came into existence with the Hell Gate Treaty of 1855. Isaac Ingalls Stevens was appointed the governor of Washington Territory in 1853. This territory consisted of areas of the later states of Washington, Idaho, and the western half of Montana. One of Stevens' tasks was to negotiate treaties with the numerous Indian tribes in the area. In order to achieve this goal, Stevens led an expedition to the Salish and Kootenai homeland in 1853. This expedition noted the favorable characteristics of the Bitterroot and Flathead River valleys, labeling them "well adapted for agriculture," "rich and arable," and "one of the most promising countries in this whole region." Stevens noted further that: "It will not be many years before the progress of settlements will establish its superiority as an agricultural region."[1] But before settlers could move in, Indians should be elsewhere. Another reason Stevens needed a treaty to extinguish Indian sovereignty in the Washington Territory was to open the way for a railroad route to the Pacific Ocean.

By July of 1855 Stevens had negotiated treaties with the Washington and Idaho tribes and moved on to Montana. At Council Grove, just west of modern-day Missoula, along the banks of Clark Fork River, starting on July 9, 1855, Stevens met with the Flathead, Kootenai, and Upper Pend d'Oreille leaders to negotiate a treaty. From the beginning, Stevens insisted on forming a single reservation for these groups, which traditionally had shared some of the same territory, but clearly were different Indian nations. Stevens had neither the time nor the patience to allow the Indian leaders to discuss the treaty provisions fully. He treated the Salish and Kootenai leaders with disrespect by calling them repeatedly "my children." While the Indians came to the council prepared to sign a treaty with the United States in order to get assistance in establishing peace with the Blackfeet, Stevens came primarily to get land cessions for money. Translation from Salish to English and from English to Salish was incompetent, and Stevens completely ignored the independence of the sub chiefs. Out of this confusion and disagreement came the Hell Gate Treaty of 1855, which provided a legal foundation for the relationship between the Confederated Salish and Kootenai Tribes and the federal government.[2]

Chiefs Victor of the Flatheads, Alexander of the Upper Pend d'Oreille, and Michelle of the Kootenai clearly expressed their desires for at least two different reservations,[3] but Stevens ignored this perspective, probably realizing that he had no authority to promise a second reservation. Tribal delegates considered themselves three different tribes, and did not want to become one on a single reservation. Flathead Red Wolf expressed these views: "I think of the three nations this [Council Grove area] belongs to the Flatheads — this is closed up by mountains. There is another place over yonder — across the mountains — that belongs to the Pend Oreilles. I do not know where the country of the Kootenays is. It is a long distance off."[4]

Victor and Alexander doubted whether one location would be large enough for all of them. Victor did not want to move to the Flathead valley and Alexander expressed that he was happy around the mission at St. Ignatius.[5] At one point, Alexander got upset over Stevens' inflexibility: "When you first talked, you talked good; now you talk sharp; you talk like a Blackfoot."[6]

Stevens could not get the chiefs' signatures until he had ambiguously promised them that the United States government would survey both the Flathead and Bitterroot River Valleys to determine which location was more suitable for Victor and the Flatheads. Stevens probably knew that the United States Congress would never allow establishment of two reservations for these three tribes.[7] The promise of a government survey of both

locations was the only concession Stevens made in the treaty negotiations. The Indians, however, had a different interpretation
of the treaty. They thought that Stevens had promised them two
reservations. Besides, their original motivation for the treaty was
to get protection from the United States against the raids of the
Blackfeet, which Stevens promised. On July 16, 1855, Stevens,
Victor, Alexander, Michelle and fifteen subchiefs signed the Hell
Gate Treaty, which became a point of contention 99 years later
during the termination struggle.

The Salish and Kootenai ceded a total of 12.8 million acres
in the treaty. Two-thirds of this territory would eventually be set
aside as national forests. Despite the treaty's weaknesses and contested purpose, it was the only legal document for the tribes on
the newly established Flathead reservation to hold on to. The
treaty allowed the tribes to protest, unsuccessfully, the allotment
of the reservation without tribal consent in 1910, and successfully, in 1954, to point out that termination of federal supervision
would break the treaty of 1855 against tribal wishes. The treaty
was indeed ambiguous. While the United States regarded the
tribes capable of making treaties, it treated them like dependent
parties. Reservation land was to be inviolable, but white settlers
were allowed to move in without penalty at the start of the twentieth century. It guaranteed the right of the Indian people to hunt
and fish in their accustomed territory, but the state of Montana,
not a party to the treaty, has often challenged this right. For Indians it was a treaty for protection: They wanted the Americans
as allies in the fight against the Blackfeet, but they also wanted to
be able to continue their traditional lifestyles.[8]

The treaty provided that the three tribes thereafter constituted one nation under the name Flathead Nation, with Victor
as the head chief. Article 1 provided for land cessions. Article
2 called for a reservation "surveyed and marked out for the exclusive use and benefit of said confederated tribes as an Indian
reservation. Nor shall any white man, excepting those in the

employment of the Indian department, be permitted to reside upon the said reservation without permission of the confederated tribes, and the superintendent and agent." Yet article 3 allowed the government to build roads through the reservation. Article 4 provided for payments for the ceded lands, and in the article 5 the United States promised to establish schools, mechanics' shop, and hospital and pay salaries to the head chiefs. The most ambiguous and contested articles were numbers 6 and 11. Article 6 referred to a United States treaty with the Omahas to imply that the Salish and Kootenai consented to individual allotments and the sale of "surplus" lands to the government.[9] Article 7 ruled that Indians should not use annuities to pay debts, and article 8 acknowledged that Indians would preserve friendly relations with all United States citizens. Article 9 stated that annuities would be withheld from those who drank alcohol, and article 10 guaranteed the reservation against any claims from the British Hudson Bay Company. Article 11 provided that the Bitterroot location was to be surveyed for the possibility that it "be set apart as a separate reservation," and, until this was done, no whites were to be allowed to settle on Salish lands in the Bitterroot Valley. The government and Congress clearly did not intend to fully fulfill this requirement, and Stevens knew they would not. Finally, article 12 provided that the treaty become a binding document upon congressional ratification, which took place in 1859.[10]

Allotment of the Flathead Indian Reservation

In 1887, Congress passed an act to allot all Indian reservations into individual parcels. Although this Dawes Act, named after its sponsor, Massachusetts Senator Henry Dawes, applied in theory to all reservations, it required passage of another, more specific bill in order to deal with a specific reservation. The opening of reservation lands to white settlement was a popular notion among white Montanans. Local and state politicians argued that the future progress of the state was linked to the availability of these lands, and that settlement would mean an economic boom to everyone. Even the Indian would be better off, once he had modified his culture to white perceptions of civilization. In reality, the idealized goals of civilization and assimilation were a poor match for individual greed and local politics.[11]

Many merchants and residents in the budding town of Missoula, just fifteen miles south of the reservation's border, were directly involved and interested in the allotment of the reservation. They eyed development and feared that settlers would otherwise go to Canada. The extension of the Northern Pacific Railroad through the Flathead Reservation was finished in 1883. A railroad right-of-way of 1,430 acres was awarded for the sum of $23,600 against the wishes of many Salish and Kootenai.[12] Missoula business interests believed that opening the reservation would bring settlers to Missoula County which grew from 2,537 residents in 1880 to 14,427 people by 1890, and add taxable wealth to the region. The local newspaper optimistically declared that: "There is room on the Flathead reservation for thousands of settlers."[13]

In 1895 the Montana legislature memorialized the United States Congress to allot the Indian lands in the state. The moving force behind the Flathead allotment was Congressman Joseph M. Dixon, a Missoula lawyer and businessman. Dixon had relatives and associates connected to reservation businesses. One of these was the Indian agent W. H. Smead, who, once accused of running cattle on the reservation, blamed selfish Indian cattlemen for wanting the land for themselves. Smead was dismissed in 1904, but the next agent Samuel Bellew, while being less corrupt, also supported allotment and manipulated reservation politics toward that goal.[14]

Dixon and his allies still needed tribal consent for allotment to occur. Government attempts to negotiate for this kind of a treaty with the Salish in 1901 had failed, when Charlo declared: "I won't sell a foot!" Dixon tried to persuade the tribal representatives: "Since it was only a matter of time until all reservations would be opened for white settlement, it was only logical, he reasoned, that the Flatheads agree to his bill."[15] Dixon would not take no for an answer. He threatened the tribe by pointing out that the Supreme Court's 1903 decision Lone Wolf vs. Hitchcock gave the United States Congress the right to pass legislation in Indian affairs as it saw fit. The Department of the Interior recommended allotment to "civilize" Indians. Still the tribal leaders remained skeptical; they did not want patents to their land. Then Dixon discovered the controversial article 6 of the 1855 Hell Gate Treaty. Using it to provide an argument that the tribe had consented to the opening of the reservation, he introduced the Flathead allotment bill in 1903. The bill sailed through Congress with the aid of Montana's Senators William Clark and Paris Gibson, and President Theodore Roosevelt signed "An act for the survey and allotment of lands now embraced within the limits of the Flathead Indian Reservation in the State of Montana, and the sale and disposal of all surplus lands after allotment" into law on April 23, 1904.[16]

The Flathead Allotment Act offered no plan for the development of Indians as individuals and it prevented their existence as a tribe. Whites soon outnumbered Indians on the reservation. The result was near disastrous for the tribal economy. Tribal members have contended that allotment was the root of reservation poverty. Tribal elder Charles McDonald recalled: "Allotment system was a sad deal . . . BIA had silly rules on issuance of patents . . . [I was] Forced to patent land, [which] later proved a mistake since I lost [the] land." Open range and the few large cattle herds were lost and fencing caused changes in tribal customs.[17] Heirship interests on allotments caused fractionalization of individual tracks and this increased the costs of establishing a clear owner and manager for the parcels and made coordination of production nearly impossible.[18] In essence, Congress had destroyed a successful ranching community. Allotment forced the

Indians into the market economy unprepared, caused forced acculturation, and the decline of old social systems including the
power of the chiefs.[19] One current tribal elder pointed to the fact
that flaws in the 1855 treaty made it possible to open the reservation for settlement. He thought that Indians were not then
ready for individual farming. The Dawes Act passed because of
assimilation, because "whites didn't understand we were a different country." He acknowledged that "if we had lawyers then, the
treaty would not have been broken."[20]

The Flathead Allotment Act resulted in the opening of the
reservation in 1910. Before that date, a final tribal roll had to be
made to determine how many Indians were entitled to an allotment. This constituted a difficult task in any case, but it became
even more so as many full bloods resisted the count. The "final"
roll of 1905 counted 2,133 Indians: 837 Pend d'Oreilles, 557
Salish, 556 Kootenai and 183 others. This roll was disputed by
all. The count of 1909 already found 2,390 Indians eligible for
an allotment for either 80 acres of farm land or 160 acres of
grazing pasture. In addition, 18,500 acres were provided for a
national bison range and 5,000 acres for a forest reserve. Combined Indian allotments were only 245,000 acres or one fifth of
the reservation. The remaining lands were opened for homestead
lottery. Eventually 4,500 homesteads were formed on 404,000
acres.[21] One quarter of them remained empty by 1920, and Congress passed an act in February 1920 to provide "Allotments to all
unallotted living children enrolled with Flathead nation." That
was about 850 children born after 1905, who got mostly worth-
less land unsuitable for farming or grazing.[22]

It seems clear that allotment in general, and particularly the
allotment of the Flathead Reservation, reduced the sovereignty
of the Salish and Kootenai government, and it can be argued
that the opening of the reservation to white settlement represented a step toward the eventual termination of the reservation.
Lorena Burgess, the leading tribal member advocating termina-

tion, thought that the meaning of the 1904 Flathead Allotment Act was to "finally and forever dissolve the Flathead Reservation and the Flathead Tribes." The act provided that after the reservation was surveyed and the assets appraised, the property was to be sold and proceeds to be divided among those appearing on the final roll. At the end of 25 years those with allotments could be released from wardship. But when, to the surprise of the government, much land remained to be sold in 1920, those 850 children were added to the roll and given allotments.[23]

The Indian New Deal

The Indian Reorganization Act (IRA) of 1934 was the central feature of the Indian New Deal. The Roosevelt administration attempted to make a fundamental change in Indian affairs. The IRA in its original form sought (1) economic rehabilitation of the Indians, principally on the land (meaning the end of allotment), (2) organization of Indian tribes for managing their own affairs, 3) civil and cultural freedom and opportunity for Indians, and (4) to settle all the existing claims the tribes had against the federal government.[24]

Senator Burton Wheeler of Montana, when introducing the IRA bill in the Senate, declared that in the long run it will be much cheaper if these Indians were given land to help make better citizens of them. This bill was a step toward the abolishment of the whole Bureau of Indian Affairs and creation of Indian self-government.[25] Representative Edgar Howard of Nebraska introduced the bill in the House of Representatives. He emphasized that Indians undeniably should have some power over their own affairs.[26] President Roosevelt spoke highly of the bill: "It is . . . a measure of justice that is long overdue . . . We can and should without further delay extend to the Indian the fundamental rights of political liberty and local self-government and the opportunities of education and economic assistance that they require in order to attain a wholesome American life."[27]

But Congress did not share the president's enthusiasm about the bill. The final version of the act did not provide for civil and cultural freedom and opportunity for Indians nor did it provide for the claims settlement. The provisions for tribal self-management were severely curtailed. The act resulted from numerous compromises that shortened the original bill's 48 pages to a mere four. One of the major provisions, section 3, authorized the secretary of the interior to restore to tribal ownership the remaining unallotted lands. Section 10 established the sum of ten million dollars as a revolving credit fund which made loans to tribes and individual Indians, and section 16 legislated for setting up new tribal governments with at least some degree of self-determination.[28]

For the first time in United States Indian policy, the government through the IRA attempted to add to the land base of reservations and to improve land already in them. At least the additional sale of Indian land came to a stop, even if the reservation land base did not increase much. Congress made meager appropriations for this initiative. The IRA also created new tribal governments, to be established by tribal option. Through that provision, the legislation managed to reaffirm the doctrine of limited sovereignty, which the tribes had exercised before the end of the treaty period in 1871. Yet the IRA left an almost unlimited power to the secretary of the interior to overrule tribal decisions and imposed a United States type of representative government on all reservations which approved IRA, whether their traditional government fitted into this formula or not. In addition, Commissioner John Collier failed to define what limits he would place on tribal power.[29] In many ways, the IRA replaced BIA officials with tribal governments as the first targets of native criticism. Indeed, tribal leaders more often than not were accused of being BIA puppets who didn't care about true Indian opinion.[30]

Former BIA employees provide some insights to the thinking behind the IRA. D'Arcy McNickle, an enrolled member of the

Confederated Salish and Kootenai Tribes, remembered the time when he was an official of the BIA during the Indian New Deal. He wrote that Congress wanted "the 'Indian business' cleaned up," but was not willing to transfer any real power to Indian tribes under the IRA. He charged that because Congress struck all the provisions of the BIA bill that gave the Indians a deciding role, the rules of bureaucracy remained intact. McNickle understood that despite serious attempts to better the Indian future, the bureaucracy still carried a heritage of colonial administration.[31]

Clearly, the IRA did not oppose assimilation altogether, as Senator Wheeler's statement demonstrated. John Collier himself admitted that the act encouraged "assimilation, not into our culture but into modern life." He concluded that "preservation and intensification of heritage are not hostile choices."[32] Whatever Collier's main objective was, in reality the IRA was essentially conservative in its nature and in its reforms. The original bill even gave tribal members the right to withdraw from their tribes in exchange for a cash compensation, an essential part of the termination bills of the 1950s.[33]

Senator Wheeler and Commissioner Collier saw the purposes of the IRA differently. By 1937 the senator had realized that the act was not moving the Native Americans towards assimilation as he had hoped. He introduced a bill to repeal the IRA.[34] The tribal representatives had seen only the original version of the bill, and when the act itself differed from this, tribal confusion became apparent. Probably the law's biggest flaw was that the tribal constitutions based on the IRA actually did not provide Indian tribes with any other governmental options other than those that were established in a Euro-American form that often was unsuitable for tribal cultures. Often Commissioner Collier chose to ignore the law's limitations and acted as if his original plans could still be enacted. Where legislative authority ended, Collier moved to implement the IRA's provisions by administrative means.[35]

Indians on the Flathead Reservation were quick to adopt a government based on the Indian Reorganization Act. They recognized that the new government, combined with new attitudes in John Collier's BIA, would give them more political power and would diminish the power of the Indian agent. In adopting a constitution and bylaws in 1935, the three major groups on the reservation, and many of the smaller groups that had settled there, became officially known as the Confederated Salish and Kootenai Tribes of the Flathead Indian Reservation. The progressiveness of these groups and their traditional willingness to adapt to the outside environment made them the first Native American community to ratify the Indian Reorganization Act.

A referendum vote was required before any tribe would become a subject to a government based on the United States model of representative government. The Indians at Flathead adopted the new tribal constitution with a margin of 549-123. Of the total number of more than 1,200 adults, 672 or 56 percent voted.[36] Superintendent L.W. Shotwell optimistically argued that those opposed to the measure voted 100 percent. He also argued that "Jealousies, personal and community rivalry, all have been submerged for the good of all."[37] Both arguments are doubtful considering the traditional Indian practice of not voting at all on a matter they dislike and the fact that the tribes hardly were then, or have been since, united. To accommodate the old chief system of government, according to which each tribe had a head chief, sub chief and several small chiefs, Salish chief Martin Charlo and Kootenai chief Paul Koostata became honorary members of the tribal council for life, bringing its membership to twelve.[38] Charlo died in 1941 and Koostata in 1947, after which the tribal council has had ten members representing districts based on old settlement patterns.[39]

Department of the Interior Solicitor Felix Cohen wrote the IRA constitutions, including the one for the Salish and Kootenai. Many past and current tribal members have pointed to the fact that the constitution is inadequate and non-democratic, giving the tribal council all the power on the reservation. The Salish and Kootenai government is not divided into branches, which was the major oversight of the draftees. The tribal council holds supreme power over tribal members in law and order and quickly established a court of Indian offenses and law and order code. Therefore the legislative and executive branches were one.[40]

The United States Congress has the ultimate authority — plenary power — over reservation affairs, which was a constant threat to the tribes and made the powers of self-government theoretical. In addition, it was hard to find a type of council that could represent all tribal members. The council was not checked by any other body than the BIA. It did not delegate and council members were blamed for nepotism, negligence, and lack of skills.[41] They were accused of representing the mixed blood population, ignoring the wishes of the full bloods and those holding on to traditional cultures. Still, many acknowledged that the IRA constitution gave Indians more control and voice in their own affairs. Charles McDonald, brother of the long-time tribal chairman Walter McDonald, argued that, thanks to the IRA, the tribes were able to get back grazing land, improve education, and accomplish other goals. Charles McDonald worked his own ranch and was employed by the tribe in various positions. He also did occasional work for the United States Forest Service.[42]

Until the reservation government was reorganized in 1935, the business committee, founded in 1909 and consisting of young progressives, competed with the chiefs. Disagreements between the old and the young leaders arose over the use of tribal resources.[43] The IRA gave tribes authority to restore timberlands and to buy additional land, which Superintendent L. W. Shotwell acknowledged was of primary importance.[44] The act gave the tribal council many powers in the management of Indian Affairs, such as rehabilitation of families, health, and education. But these powers did not come automatically; at first the council was informal, and did not make broader policy. It worked on routine domestic tasks while the BIA still controlled major reservation affairs. Yet the council was carefully watched by the tribal members, so that it would follow traditions of individual autonomy and consensus.[45] Even as Commissioner Collier did not seem fully to trust Indians for their own governance, the ultimate power rested on the superintendent, the commissioner of Indian affairs, and the secretary of the interior. All council decisions had to be confirmed by the secretary of the interior, effectively leaving the tribe self-governing in name only.[46] After gaining more self-confidence and experience, the tribal council started taking a bigger role in reservation affairs, particularly in the 1950s.

The 1935 constitution stipulated that enrollment required residence on the reservation which thereby excluded children born to tribal members living off the reservation. The constitution gave the tribal council the power to propose ordinances governing future membership.[47]

Termination Appears

The first proposals to dissolve specialized government services to Indians appeared during World War II. Indians' success, both on the battlefields and in the factories, made many congressmen and bureaucrats deem them ready to handle their own affairs. Many Indians, especially mixed-bloods, shared this view and believed that federal trust restrictions hindered their progress. Many members of the Confederated Salish and Kootenai Tribes shared this viewpoint. However, many bureaucrats misinterpreted this activism; they believed that all Indians wanted assimilation. Indians' dedication and involvement during the war was not an accurate barometer of their readiness for assimilation. The federal government inaccurately assumed that assimilation was occurring despite serious discrimination in localities where a large number of Indians resided.[48]

The appropriations committees of Congress used threatened or real cuts in the BIA budget as a weapon to push for assimilation. Congress forced the gradual change of bureau policy towards assimilationist goals. The main principles of the termination policy can be found in a Senate Committee of Indian Affairs report as early as 1943. Senate Report No. 310 responded to the BIA's appropriation request for the year 1944. Its 33 recommendations included the elimination of all federal control of law and order in the reservations, the freeing of Indians without trust property from federal wardship, the transfer of the responsibility for Indian education to the states, the elimination of all Indian census rolls, the transfer of all Indian hospitals to the U.S. Public Health Service, and the end of land purchases in federal trust for Indians. These same ideas all appear in the termination laws. According to the report, all these things could be achieved in one to three years, if Indian property were released from federal trust and submitted to taxes.[49] The main objectives thus included cutting government expenses and releasing "surplus" Indian land. Congressional critics complained federal Indian administration was expensive and ineffective because reservation conditions remained deplorable despite a hundred years of BIA administration. They did not want Indians' special status to be unduly prolonged.[50]

The House Committee on Indian Affairs also conducted wide-ranging investigations into Indian affairs in 1944. These hearings did not criticize the bureau as severely as had the Senate committee, but the tone of their deliberations certainly supported a version of termination. Even Commissioner Collier, tired of criticism, asked for this investigation in order to "find out how many of the Indians, here and now, can be relieved of Federal supervision, or relieved after certain definable intermediate steps."[51] Some congressmen took Collier's words as a suggestion that some Indians were close to terminating their relationship with the federal government and just needed some encouragement.[52]

As a result of this investigation the House committee published a report in which it concluded that Indian integration had slowed down due to inadequate economic and educational opportunities, inadequate guidance, and overly strict regulations. The committee recommended: (1) setting up an Indian Claims Commission to settle Indian claims, (2) universal education where the role of native language would be secondary, and (3) encouraging competent Indians to leave the reservations. The United States needed to bring freedom and opportunity to Indians before the nation could enter the "court of world opinion."[53]

Continuing attempts to repeal the IRA provided another means to hamper the BIA's work. In 1944, Senate bill 1218 to repeal the IRA and the Senate Committee on Indian Affairs report which accompanied the bill, attacked the provisions of the act and its implementation, finding nothing good in either one of them. The report argued that the IRA had been passed against Indian wishes. The BIA's propaganda machine had made unsupported promises and used pressure to attain Indians' votes. Internal strife within the tribes resulted. No greater degree of tribal self-determination had taken place. Tribes had only as much control as the bureau wanted them to have. The report concluded that "Any valuable function of the Indian Reorganization Act is a duplication of a better justified function of some other unit or division of government."[54]

An immediate sign of the post-war policy change came with the creation of the U.S. Indian Claims Commission (ICC) in 1946. The ICC was to finally handle all the claims the Indian tribes had against the United States government over the lands taken, either through treaties or executive order, without proper compensation. The Meriam Report of 1928 had recommended taking care of Indian claims because they were "a serious impediment to progress . . . Until these claims are out of the way, not much can be expected of Indians who are placing their faith in them." The report staff argued that a special commission should be created to study those remaining claims.[55] Endorsed by the Meriam Report, the Indian Claims Commission bill was first introduced in Congress in 1933 as a part of the Indian New Deal. Commissioner Collier urged the passage of a bill creating a special court of Indian affairs to finally solve all Indian claims in the shortest possible time.[56]

The bills sailed through the Senate practically without discussion, but failed to gain a full hearing in the House. The opposition claimed that lawyers would be the true beneficiaries, not the Indians.[57] By 1946, when the bill to create the Indian Claims Commission finally passed, the political climate had changed. By then it could truly be seen as being a part of termination policy. Like other post-war programs it was motivated by the overall policy of eliminating the Indian as an unassimilated minority within American society. Congress never seriously considered giving the commission a mandate to award land compensation (to give land back to Indians), which was what the Indians wanted and really would have helped ease reservation poverty. Indian input in the formulation and operation of the claims process never became reality. As persistent claims seemed to be a hindrance to cultural integration and weighed on the national conscience in the Cold War battles for moral authority, clearing off this obstacle to Indian freedom seemed to make sense. Eliminating claims would lead the way to assimilating Indians, and put many tribes on a self-sustaining basis.[58]

Land, indeed, was central to the creation of the Indian Claims Commission. As one scholar correctly points out, "the government sought a means by which to quiet title to millions of acres of land today held by non-Indians; it hoped that the claims process would wash clean the government's soiled credibility and that claims judgments would distribute sufficient but not exorbitant funds, on a onetime basis, to thousands of Indians who, in turn, would benefit in some small way."[59] But Indians were disappointed in the process. And although the Indian Claims

Commission promised an erosion of federal power and provided means to assimilate Indians, its creation actually contradicted the government's policy of reduced spending. The idea was to spend money now in order to save in the long run.[60] The commission's terminationist agenda became clearer when the chief termination-ist Arthur Watkins lost his Senate seat in 1958 and was promptly appointed a chief commissioner to the ICC the next year. Indeed the speed and efficiency of award judgments increased after Wat-kins' appointment.[61] Overall, the Indian Claims Commission was a rather ineffective institution. Despite constant efforts to re-peal it and cut its funding, Congress continued its existence until 1978. It did not turn out to be an automatic jackpot for Indians. Of the 850 original claims, less than one half brought an award. The successful claims totaled some 818 million dollars.[62]

President Truman nominated Dillon S. Myer the Commis-sioner of Indian Affairs in early 1950. In recommending Myer, Secretary of the Interior Oscar Chapman did not consult Ameri-can Indian leaders or organizations because he questioned the advisability of appointing an Indian as commissioner.[63] During World War II Myer had served as director of the War Relocation Authority, a temporary agency which interned Japanese-Ameri-cans from the West Coast in ten inland camps and relocated them to various locations after the war. Ironically, Myer perceived his job as Commissioner of Indian Affairs as the duty to relocate Indians from reservations to cities. Truman also chose Myer be-cause he would follow the congressional policy of terminating federal supervision of Indian affairs. To decrease the bureau's in-ternal dissension, Myer fired old Collier-era employees and hired new employees who had worked with him in the War Relocation Authority.[64]

Myer agreed with the congressional movement to trans-fer BIA services, such as health care, to other federal and state agencies or to tribal governments. He emphasized the need to carry out this transfer in close cooperation with Indians. Yet he emphasized to his staff that even if Indians did not consent to his policies, they should be carried out anyway. Myer argued that the BIA should not continue providing services to Indians if some other agency could do the job better.[65] The commissioner emphasized Indian training, placement, and relocation away from poverty on reservations. Yet those who chose to remain on the reservation also needed economic, political and social development. He admitted that there could be no trusteeship without paternalism. Myer realized the BIA's dilemma. On the one hand, it was trying to encourage Indians to take over responsibility in the management of their own affairs; and on the other hand, it was saddled with the responsibility of protecting Indian properties.[66] Myer tried to solve this dilemma by concentrating on the transfer of responsibility and ignoring treaties and protection of the property.

During the congressional impasse over termination legislation which lasted until 1953, Myer managed to start withdrawal through administrative means. He initiated federal assistance to relocate tribal members by opening placement centers in western and midwestern cities. Myer centralized BIA's power structure to gain more control and to take power away from the reservation superintendents. He ordered every bureau agency to start preparing termination programs and submit them to him. These 1952 reports were then used as a basis for termination legislation. Indian opinions or actual local conditions were not considered in the bureau plans unless they pointed to the direction Myer wanted.[67]

Myer emphasized that any minority group should be integrated as quickly as possible. He closely followed the wishes of the congressional terminationists.[68] These men, all from western states, included Senator Hugh Butler of Nebraska, Senators Patrick McCarran and George Malone from Nevada, Senator Arthur Watkins from Utah, and Representatives E. Y. Berry of South Dakota and Wesley D'Ewart of Montana. They occupied positions mostly in public lands and Indian affairs committees and subcommittees. Even if few of these men's propositions for federal withdrawal in Indian affairs passed before 1953, Congress did cut back some of the Indian Bureau's appropriations. This resulted in reductions of some of the bureau's services on reservations, especially health care and the revolving loan fund of the Indian Reorganization Act. Groups favoring the release of tribal lands from federal restrictions so that they could be put under taxation hid their real intentions by arguing that Indians should be allowed to make their own business decisions and possible mistakes. Western congressmen argued, in the name of self-determination, that Indians should be cut loose from federal restrictions to make their own decisions without interference or help from the federal government. That influential factions on reservations and Indian lobby groups had argued that they wanted more responsibility in reservation affairs added fuel to this rhetoric, even if the sides generally disagreed in how this self-determination should work in reality. Yet Commissioner Myer argued that Indians should not be allowed to make preventable mistakes in running their own affairs as long as they were under government supervision, even if it were in the name of self-determination.[69]

A leading spokesman for termination after 1952 and a vocal representative of the conservative backlash to President Truman's Fair Deal policies, Senator Watkins believed that everyone should achieve their goals without government assistance, regardless of circumstances. He thought that cultural values and background made little difference to individual chances.[70] Having practiced law in Vernal, Utah, Watkins was elected senator in 1947. He gladly served as Indian Affairs Subcommittee Chairman and personally dominated the termination hearings in 1954. He argued that his only goal could be "freedom for the Indian."[71] Watkins also had a strongly pro-business orientation and belief in "rugged individualism." Keeping Indian lands in federal trust yielded

Senator Arthur Watkins

Source: Shot 2, MSS C400, photo number 19097, Utah State Historical Society, Salt Lake City, Utah.

the fundamental reason for the Indians' slow rate of "progress." He also believed that Indian opposition to termination stemmed from the desire to avoid paying taxes, conveniently ignoring the fact that Indians paid taxes on everything but their land if it remained in trust status. If the government abandoned its commitment to Indian assimilation, the development of reservation resources could be lost. Watkins arrogantly believed he knew what was best for the Indians: "They want the guardianship to continue; but in my opinion it would be in their best interests for them to be on their own." He did not bother to consult the targets of his policies nor listen to their objections.[72]

Western land and water interests played an important part in the termination movement. Terminationists did not directly mention the significance of Native resources, but their relative silence did not diminish the importance of the fact that the economic boom in the west after World War II increased the need to develop reservation resources. Senator Hugh Butler, for example, believed that Indians had not lost any of the ninety million acres as the result of the Allotment Act of 1887, but rather had "sold it." Besides, he suggested, they had plenty of land left because they were leasing it out to non-Indians. He completely ignored the realities of the past land losses. Butler supported oil, timber, grazing, fishing, hunting, and real estate industries, which hoped for the liquidation of Indian reservations.[73]

Representative E. Y. Berry chaired the House Indian Affairs Subcommittee and joined Senator Watkins in a combined effort to terminate a number of Indian reservations in 1954. He, too, was a conservative opponent of the New Deal, who had a laissez-faire, pro-business orientation and believed in "rugged individualism." He viewed reservations as the last exploitable frontier regions. A resident of McLaughlin, South Dakota, a community located on the Standing Rock Sioux Reservation, Berry later toned down his views in order to court Indian votes to get re-elected. Still he argued that the IRA and reservation governments were socialistic and he advocated policies, such as relocation, to eliminate the need for the BIA at some future time.[74]

These western congressmen got support from the Governors' Interstate Indian Council (GIIC), which represented fifteen governors in midwestern and western states with large Indian populations. Montana Governor John Bonner argued that because of the critical situation existing concerning the tribal and landless Indians, he and Governor Luther Youngdahl of Minnesota organized the GIIC because they felt that states should take action to solve the problems.[75] The GIIC developed an agenda which emphasized states' rights and rapid economic development in the west. It advocated the transfer of BIA services to the states, which, the council argued, could operate them effectively. Relocation should be pursued and termination dates set for most tribes.[76] The governors emphasized the need to help Indians to help themselves, therefore needless restrictions should be removed and education, vocational training, and employment opportunities improved. Treaty claims should be settled as they kept Indians on the reservations. The GIIC concluded that the long range goal must be full equality for Indians without any special privileges, but Indian cooperation was needed to achieve that goal.[77]

The ability of Watkins, Butler, and Berry to dominate congressional policies on Indian affairs reflected the low priority that Indian affairs had in Congress. Subcommittee reports often got a rubber stamp treatment unless someone rose in opposition. Party politics had little significance; votes on Indian bills went along regional lines.[78] Yet the opposition of a few congressmen could also defeat the bills. Therefore an Indian organization or a tribe which could convince a congressman of the harmful effect of a particular policy to Indians could persist and defeat that policy. The Salish and Kootenai proved this during the termination battle.

On August 1, 1953, Congress passed the House Concurrent Resolution (HCR) 108. The resolution stated Indians should
be made "subject to the same laws and entitled to the same privileges and responsibilities as are applicable to other citizens of
the United States." Further: "at the earliest possible time, all the
Indian tribes . . . should be freed from federal supervision and
control and from all disabilities and limitations specially applicable to Indians."[79] HCR 108 passed with minimal attention and
discussion in the Republican controlled 83rd Congress, where
the few interested congressmen viewed Indian reservations as
un-American strongholds for foreign ideas and political systems.
Although not an act, HCR 108 provided an affirmative step towards termination legislation. The congressmen responsible for
this resolution — Representative William Harrison of Wyoming
and Senator Henry Jackson of Washington — inaccurately and
misleadingly implied that Indians were not citizens and therefore
not subject to the laws of the United States.[80]

Given Senator Watkins' views on Indian affairs, it was no
surprise that HCR 108 became a direct guideline for the termination policy. The committee considered bills to terminate the
federal supervision of the Utes of Utah, Texas Indians, tribes in
western Oregon, the Klamaths of Oregon, California Indians, the
Menominees of Wisconsin, the Salish and Kootenai of Montana,
the Seminoles of Florida, the Makah Tribe of Washington, the Indians of Nevada, the Sac and Fox, the Kickapoo and Potawatomi
tribes of Kansas and Nebraska, and the Turtle Mountain Chippewas of North Dakota. That these particular states and tribes were
picked for immediate termination of federal supervision was not
an accident. Termination advocates expected that these states
wanted to assume the responsibility for Indian affairs and that
these tribes indeed were ready for taking on the responsibility of
running the reservations as corporate entities. Most of them were
considered ready, because they had substantial resources.

Born in Worcester, Massachusetts, in 1889, Wesley D'Ewart worked for the United States Forest Service and ranched before being elected to the United States House of Representatives from Montana in 1945. In 1952 Republican D'Ewart introduced three bills to confer the jurisdiction of several Indian reservations to states. In the House Subcommittee on Indian Affairs hearings on one of his bills, H.R. 459, D'Ewart stated that these bills were needed because of legal twilight zones within many reservations. Commissioner Myer agreed with Congressman D'Ewart. He stated that before any state assumed jurisdiction on Indian reservations, Indians should be consulted but their consent was not necessary.[81]

Commenting on D'Ewart's bills, the Confederated Salish and Kootenai tribal council chairman Walter McDonald said that he had always leaned toward law enforcement by the state.[82] Yet the tribal council disapproved H.R. 459, citing racial prejudice in the state of Montana.[83] Although D'Ewart's bills did not pass, they formed a precedent to Public Law 280 of 1953, which allowed state jurisdiction in reservations. Montana Indians in general opposed PL 280, pointing out that it did not require consultation with the tribes affected. Good law enforcement was dependent upon the cooperation and confidence of the citizens concerned; both were lacking in this law.[84]

Public Law 280 authorized the states of California, Nebraska, Minnesota (except for the Red Lake Reservation), Oregon (except for the Warm Springs Reservation), and Wisconsin (except for the Menominee Reservation) to exercise civil and criminal jurisdiction over all Indian lands within their boundaries. Other states could assume the same authority through agreements with tribal governments or through amending their state constitutions. Many states used one of these methods to assume jurisdiction on one or more of the reservations within the state's borders. Montana required a constitutional amendment. Public Law 280 reflected termination philosophy by transferring

Representative Wesley A. D'Ewart

Source: Hester Studio, Billings, Montana, photographer, PAc2008-57.2, Photographic Archives, Montana Historical Society, Helena, Montana.

federal responsibilities on reservation law and order to states. It was also a federal cost-cutting measure. Unfortunately, PL 280 did not require Indian consent for the transfer. Tribes opposed the measure for that reason. The law offered a compromise between abandoning some Indians to the states and maintaining others as federally protected wards.[85]

In 1954 Senator Watkins and Representative Berry organized Indian Affairs subcommittees for joint hearings on termination. Hearings followed a familiar pattern: Senator Watkins argued for termination because, according to him, tribes did not pay taxes, their progress was slowed because of federal supervision, and reservations were communist strongholds. If state representatives opposed termination of tribes within their boundaries, the bills did not pass.[86]

Altogether the 14-man House Indian Affairs Subcommittee of the 83rd Congress alone or jointly with the Senate Indian Affairs Subcommittee heard 472 witnesses in Washington and 22 states for 147 hours. The result was 3,292 pages of printed transcripts. Witnesses represented 115 bands or tribes.[87] All in all, withdrawal bills on six of these twelve tribal groups (Menominee, Klamath, western Oregon, Alabama-Coushatta of Texas, Mixed-blood Utes and Southern Paiutes of Utah) passed in 1954. Six more termination bills on new groups eventually passed, the latest in 1962. The total Indian population on the terminated reservations was 13,263.[88] The termination policy continued through to the early 1960s, when the original termination acts took effect and the last ones passed, but the tide for termination started to turn in 1954, when many tribes managed to defeat the legislation affecting their reservations.

Chapter 2

Termination at Flathead:
The Tribal Debate

This chapter deals with the Confederated Salish and Kootenai Tribes' internal debate of the advantages and disadvantages of
termination. The tribes were far from unified, but several issues
loomed large in the ensuing debate. The tribal council argued
that tribal land should remain free from taxation, the more traditional elders needed further assistance, and treaty obligations
should not be severed. On the other hand, by World War II it
was clear that a significant number of tribal members were willing
to cut their relationship with the tribes. When the termination
policy developed, it was not surprising that these tribal members,
who wanted full liquidation and distribution of tribal assets, saw
their chance to cash in on their share of tribal property. This effort ultimately failed because of the unified effort of the tribal
council, which, with the support of a majority of tribal members,
Montana's congressional delegation and state officials, managed
to keep the reservation and tribal lands intact.

Earlier than anyone on or off the reservation, Lorena Burgess in the early 1940s argued for liquidation of tribal assets.
She influenced the full-blood hereditary chief Paul Charlo, who
wanted to get an act passed so that the tribal members wishing to
retain their membership could do so; retention should be entirely
voluntary. He agreed with Burgess that the tribal council did not
represent tribal members.[1] Ironically, at that time the Bureau of
Indian Affairs (BIA) disagreed. Assistant Commissioner William
Zimmerman responded that patents in fee would result in a loss

Lorena Burgess
Top: As a young woman. Bottom: In her later years.

Source: Top: Sandra Burgess Miller, Plains, Montana.
Bottom: Confederated Salish and Kootenai Tribes,

of land and that the council had done a very good job in managing tribal affairs.[2]

Lorena Burgess kept on lamenting that "the Wheeler-Howard Reorganization Act is a separate government within a state."
She contended that those tribal members who had left the reservation for outside work were wise and had learned to stand on
their own feet.[3] The Senate Committee on Indian Affairs organized hearings on S. 1311, a bill to remove restrictions on Indian
property, in 1944. Burgess, then a tribal council member, joined
twenty other Salish Kootenai tribal members to announce their
support for this bill: "we are now justly entitled to a full and final
accounting in all our affairs with the Government, and that we
receive payment in full of whatever is due us." They considered
the entire agency system unjust and destructive.[4]

Prompted by Superintendent L. W. Shotwell, the tribal
council in 1944 requested full tribal control of resources and removal of BIA supervision for a period of five years to test tribal
ability to run their own affairs. In the 1944 House Committee on
Indian Affairs hearings, tribal chairman Steve DeMers admitted
that the council was a puppet for the BIA. He wanted the tribes
to have the opportunity to manage the reservation affairs without
government regulations. However, he acknowledged that if tribal
resources were taxed, foreclosures would be the result.[5] Other Salish witnesses argued that mixed-blood council members were not
helping the poorer full-bloods, but did everything for personal
gain. Assistant Commissioner William Zimmerman disagreed
with these critics; he repeated his belief that the Flathead tribal
council was doing an excellent job.[6]

Steve DeMers was born and raised on the Flathead Reservation. An electrician by training, he later moved to Butte,
Montana. Along with another tribal member, D'Arcy McNickle,
DeMers was on the eight-person executive council of the new-
ly-founded National Congress of American Indians (NCAI) in
1944.[7] In 1953 the Montana Inter-Tribal Policy Board endorsed

Steve DeMers

Source: Confederated Salish and Kootenai Tribes,
Pablo, Montana.

DeMers for Commissioner of Indian Affairs.[8] In 1960 DeMers was the executive director and Walter McDonald the president of the Northwest Affiliated Tribes, a consortium of tribal councils in the Pacific Northwest.[9] DeMers certainly was not suggesting the withdrawal of tribal lands from the federal trust. However, the advocates of termination would take the tribal arguments for the removal of restrictions and increased self-management as signs that the Salish and Kootenai tribes had requested permanent withdrawal of federal supervision.

S. 1311 did not pass, but in 1947, immediately following Acting Commissioner Zimmerman's testimony, per congressional request, of tribal readiness for termination, Senator Hugh Butler introduced nine withdrawal bills. One of these was S.1682: "To remove restrictions on the property and moneys belonging to the individual enrolled members of the Flathead Indian Tribe in Montana, to provide for the liquidation of tribal property and distribution of the proceeds thereof, to confer complete citizenship upon such Indians and other purposes."[10] Zimmerman had placed the Flathead Reservation in part one of his list, those ready for immediate termination, in part because it contained resources. A local newspaper speculated that Zimmerman may have done it because the tribes had shown their ability to govern themselves or because tribal members had never voiced any real opposition to government proposals.[11] Some Salish elders in the 1990s asserted as fact that their reservation was chosen for immediate termination because they had resources — land and dam sites — which could be opened just as had happened with the allotment.[12] Both S. 1311 and S. 1682 were introduced without the Flathead tribal council's input. These attempts to benefit a few individuals did not get a serious hearing.

In a response to Lorena Burgess' inquiry, BIA employee D'Arcy McNickle replied that Senator Butler's bills "are not to be taken too seriously." He suggested that Burgess discuss the withdrawal with Ruth Bronson of the NCAI, as countering efforts to liquidate federal responsibility was "one of the original reasons for organizing the Congress [NCAI]." McNickle feared that the government would have to withdraw for lack of funds because the United States Congress had cut funding in Indian affairs. He observed that the people shouting the loudest about turning the Indians loose cared not a "hoot" about Indians, but were intensely interested in their timber and minerals.[13]

BIA officials, McNickle among them, were aware that the congressional mood had changed, and realized that proposals to cut federal expenses on Indian affairs would be coming. William A. Brophy, who followed John Collier as the BIA chief, sent field representative McNickle to touch base with tribal councils regarding future changes. At the Flathead Reservation, McNickle met with the tribal council in September 1946. At that time Eneas Granjo, a 64-year old ¾ Salish rancher/farmer from Arlee, chaired the tribal council.[14] McNickle urged the council to develop a plan for withdrawal utilizing its IRA charter for self-determination. He feared that Congress might otherwise begin withdrawal without tribal consent and input. McNickle suggested that the tribal council operate independently by taxing tribal business and personal property. Tribal council members were not willing to start withdrawal planning as the idea was new to them. Tribal leaders feared that the administrative expenses would be too high and pointed to the legal and moral obligations of the Hell Gate Treaty of 1855, which the withdrawal would ignore. The federal government had yet to provide adequate schools as promised in the treaty. Yet the council did appoint a special committee to study McNickle's recommendations. This committee concluded that the tribes favored the status quo because they feared losing control of tribal resources under a business plan with a manager, possibly an outsider, in charge.[15]

Senator Butler's bill S. 1682 to terminate the Flathead Reservation provoked immediate discussion in the tribal council meetings. Congressman Wesley D'Ewart attended one of the council meetings. He claimed that he was not familiar with the Butler bill. D'Ewart argued that the House Committee on Public Lands, on which he had a seat, was not willing to liquidate any tribe without its consent. He concluded that individual Indians could have a chance, with a mutual agreement with the tribe, to withdraw, but contended that not all Indians in the state of Montana would withdraw. Tribal secretary Phil Hamel spoke for the council; he thought that the tribes could take over the management of their affairs under certain conditions. D'Ewart acknowledged that treaty obligations must be considered and that there should be quite a few informal discussions before any bills were drafted. This Senator Butler had not done.[16]

Even before Senator Butler introduced his bills to terminate nine reservations, Congress cut appropriations to the Indian Service. For the fiscal year 1946, Congress reduced the Flathead agency appropriations for relief and rehabilitation of needy Indians from $450,000 to $375,000 and authorized the tribes to use their own funds for the same purpose in the amount of $75,000, a net reduction of $25,000. These cuts prompted the BIA to recommend limiting eligibility to include only those truly needy and totally dependent.[17] With these cuts, Congress had asked that the Salish and Kootenai tribes become completely independent in five years. Council member Henry Matt, despite his earlier comments on problems with the Wheeler-Howard Act, did not believe that the tribes could be ready in five years or even ten years. Superintendent C. C. Wright thought it might be a good thing for the tribes to manage their own affairs if this goal could be accomplished gradually over a period of ten years.[18]

D'Arcy McNickle did not doubt that a gradual acculturation and lessening of the BIA's control were forthcoming. He wanted tribes to prepare for this outcome and fully participate in planning a gradual withdrawal. But he opposed any plan which lacked adequate tribal input and preparation time. Although born on the Flathead Reservation, McNickle was a one-quarter

D'Arcy McNickle

Source: D'Arcy McNickle Papers, Box 34, Folder 290, Newberry Library,
Chicago, Illinois.

Cree/Métis whose father was a white rancher. He had attended Chemawa boarding school in Salem, Oregon, from 1913 to 1916, an experience which showed in his novels. Able to speak only English, McNickle was influenced by both white and Indian cultures. Born in 1904, just before the allotment of the reservation, McNickle had been assigned a parcel of land, which he sold in 1925 in order to attend Oxford University in England.[19]

McNickle worked for the Bureau of Indian Affairs from 1936 until 1952, but he resigned because he was convinced that termination of Indian reservations was morally wrong and because the government was unable to develop a more constructive policy. He opposed Commissioner Dillon Myer's vision of reservations as temporary relocation centers administered insensitively by bureaucrats. Based on his life experience, McNickle knew that no administrative bureaucracy could create an effective policy unless Native Americans contributed. He finally rejected the idea of assimilation as inevitable in 1957.[20] This may have been in part due to the termination policies and particularly to tribal opposition to the forced withdrawal of federal supervision.

McNickle wrote novels and wrote as well about the place of American Indians in American history in numerous articles and several scholarly books. He argued that the United States trusteeship of Indian lands had evolved based on mutual consent and that the consensus should not be abandoned. McNickle agreed with those who believed that better education, rehabilitation, and less discrimination would offer Indians the option to move to urban areas without force.[21] He knew that before integration of a people could take place, a process of acculturation must be set in motion. This process was gradual and resisted outside pressures, such as congressional legislation. If Indians did not support this process, McNickle predicted, termination policies would fail.[22] McNickle called for properly trained BIA employees and recalled that an attempt in this direction had been made during the John Collier administration with the hiring of anthropologists. He charged that instead of solving Indian overpopulation on reservations by adding to their land base, Commissioner Myer had chosen to relocate Indians to cities, thereby pleasing the non-Indian West, which was all too anxious to place Indian lands under taxation.[23]

Lorena Burgess' activities among Montana Indians angered many individuals. Thomas Main, vice chairman of the Fort Belknap tribal council and regional secretary for Montana for the National Congress of American Indians, complained to Burgess about a questionnaire she had handed out to Montana Indians. He labeled the questions as loaded and biased in favor of termination. Burgess wanted people to answer yes or no to 129 questions, including: "Do you think that as long as you are designated incompetent WARDS of the government you should be made to serve in the ARMED SERVICES?" and "Do you believe in communal property?" Main felt that nobody wanted to answer these questions yes or no because Burgess was going to present the answers to the Governors' Interstate Indian Council, to which she was a Montana delegate. The GIIC could then declare that Indians were either ready for termination or unpatriotic. Main argued that governors treated Indians in a paternalistic way and complained that these types of questionnaires threatened tribal government, property, loan funds, oil and water rights, and tax exemptions.[24]

In March 1950, tribal chairman Walter McDonald and council member Walter Morigeau met with the House of Representatives Indian Affairs Subcommittee regarding a proposal to abolish BIA area offices. Chairman McDonald said that the tribes paid the salary of "seven or eight" BIA employees and used their own funds to supplement hospitalization, rehabilitation, and education of tribal members to cover the shortfall created by the federal government's failure to fulfill treaty provisions. Tribal funding of some of its services prompted Congressman D'Ewart to note that the Salish and Kootenai were advanced tribes and would get their independence as soon as they wanted it. Morigeau promptly stated that they did not ask for their independence.[25] Walter Morigeau elaborated on tribal administrative and welfare expenses further in the first Montana Indian Affairs Conference in 1951. He declared that the Salish and Kootenai tribes carried ninety percent of their administration, paid $40,000 for hospitalization, paid for their own law and order, and one half of the welfare expenses, the other half being carried by county governments.[26]

Walter McDonald served as the tribal chairman through the 1950s and much of the 1960s and directed the confederated tribes through one of the most decisive periods in their history. A descendant of Angus McDonald, the Scottish trader, the St. Ignatius rancher was born in 1910. He owned 720 acres, most of it grazed. In 1949, he owned 97 head of cattle, 11 horses, 15 lambs and 40 chickens.[27] He was one of those mixed-blood well-to-do businessmen who were criticized for having too much power, yet it largely was due to his guidance that the Flathead Reservation was not terminated in the 1950s. Some current tribal elders admit that the tribal council, and specifically Walter McDonald, did a fine job in opposing termination by pointing out the dismal effects withdrawal of federal supervision would have on the tribal people and the region due to the rise in welfare cases and loss of land.[28]

As tribal member Ronald Trosper noted, the degree of Indian "blood," itself an Anglo-American measure to determine tribal membership, proved important during the termination struggle. As congressional advocates emphasized how "white" many Indians looked, a low degree of Indian blood could make tribes appear assimilated and therefore ready for termination. Those tribal leaders who fought termination at Flathead enacted a new rule for enrollment in 1951.[29] Tribal Ordinance 10A limited enrollment to those of ¼ Indian blood or more. This rule replaced Tribal Ordinance 4A of 1946, which had provided

Walter McDonald

Source: Confederated Salish and Kootenai Tribes,
Pablo, Montana.

for enrollment of those of $^1/_{16}$ Indian blood or more. Both ordinances amended article two of the 1935 constitution, which
had not specified any blood requirements for enrollment, to ensure the maintenance of a higher degree of Indian blood among
the membership.[30] This arrangement might have been a reaction
to arguments made by some tribal members. Henry Matt complained about the "white Indians" in the five-member executive
committee of the tribal council. He declared that those with $^1/_8$ or
less Indian blood should be declared non-Indians.[31] The enrollment rule was modified again in 1960 to form the present criteria
for membership. To become a member one had to have $^1/_4$ Salish
or Kootenai blood and be born on the reservation. Nevertheless,
the tribal council can adopt members. Tribal membership could
be lost due to moving abroad, as D'Arcy McNickle found out
after accepting a professorship in the Anthropology Department
of the University of Saskatchewan at Regina in 1966.[32]

When the congressional mood to terminate reservations
reappeared in 1952 after a brief hiatus, a Special Subcommittee on Indian Affairs, headed by Representative William Henry
Harrison of Wyoming, attempted to discern the tribes' capability of handling their own affairs. In Resolution 89 the House
approved Ohio Representative Frank Bow's suggestions for the
subcommittee's duties. The subcommittee was obligated to list
tribes ready for full management of their own affairs, provide
proposals for termination legislation, and find areas where the
Indian Bureau services could be cut or ended.[33]

The House Committee on Interior and Insular Affairs did
not publish the subcommittee report until the fall of 1954, after
the termination hearings for most tribes had concluded. Therefore
its significance for termination legislation could be questioned,
but it clearly showed how determined the Indian Affairs committees were to pursue termination legislation. The committee
members found it impossible to poll Indian opinion because of
the lack of tribal newspapers or other representative voices. They

concluded that the most active and advanced Indian tribes were the most reluctant to sever ties to their federal trustee. The subcommittee recommended the transfer of educational activities and law and order from the Indian Bureau to the states and the transfer of Indian health and welfare activities to the federal Department of Health, Education, and Welfare. Indians should be given eligibility to handle their own property. Significantly, the committee argued that if Acting Commissioner Zimmerman's criteria of tribal readiness were taken literally, eternal roadblocks would appear on the way to termination. Committee members contended that entire tribes had asked for termination.[34]

The subcommittee obtained its information largely from a questionnaire it sent to the BIA agencies. It concluded that the Salish and Kootenai tribes were qualified to manage their own affairs immediately. Yet the Flathead agency's answers to the questionnaire showed that the Indian Bureau, to say the least, had mixed feelings about the withdrawal of federal supervision. The agency staff reported that tribal members were largely competent, but not wholly capable of managing their own affairs. They would be able if they worked through a governing body such as a tribal corporation. The only distinguishing factor between the tribal members and the whites in the area, the Indian Bureau contended, was the small percentage of full-bloods who had not yet adapted to the life and social customs of the surrounding white communities. The tribes already operated working enterprises, such as a recreation center built around a hot springs, which yielded relatively high income. The tribes provided their own health services and law and order for tribal members. All the children went to public schools. The bureau concluded that life would "unquestionably" go on just the same if the government completely withdrew its services. Only those full-bloods would need some time to adapt. To the BIA field representative it appeared that the majority of tribal members did not feel any negative connotations in the term "wardship." On the other hand, many tribal members would like to see tribal resources and funds divided to "get theirs." A high degree of intermarriage with whites had particularly increased tribal readiness for termination. Yet the BIA did not consider the tribes ready for complete withdrawal within the specified time limit.[35]

Intermarriage had been common at Flathead for a century and had resulted in relatively low amounts of Indian blood among tribal members. In 1952, out of 4,213 tribal members, only 292 or seven percent were listed as full-bloods, and another 1,247 or thirty percent were at least of one-half Indian blood. Almost two-thirds, then, were less than half-blood Indians.[36] Degree of Indian blood had a major significance in the termination debate. Eneas Conko, a full-blood Pend d'Oreille tribal member, believed that the problem lay "between the breeds and the full-bloods." The "breeds" were educated and safe because they were "mostly white anyway," believed Conko. Where the mixed-bloods would make it, the full-bloods would be in trouble.[37] Despite the arguments of Paul Charlo criticizing the Indian Reorganization Act, it appeared clear that full-bloods were afraid of termination. Many had lived through the allotment period and feared additional treaty abrogations. Pierre Adams spoke for them in 1948 arguing that the full-bloods wished to remain government wards.[38] The full-bloods expressed their nearly unanimous support when the tribes sent a delegation to congressional hearings to oppose the termination bill.[39] Many current tribal elders claimed that mixed-bloods, either those under ½ Indian blood or of marginal Indian blood but still enrolled, wanted to liquidate their share of tribal assets. Many of them had no ties to the reservation and had not been raised with traditional cultural values.[40]

According to the latest information available regarding termination, in 1952 111 or one-tenth of Salish-Kootenai families were totally dependent on aid or tribal welfare funds. Reservation resources could provide a livelihood for all but 132 of the resident Indian families. Tribal trust lands consisted of 644,000 acres, of which 200,000 acres were individually owned and 474,000 acres were forest lands. The tribe's total annual income for fiscal year 1952 was $800,000, consisting of $550,000 worth of timber sales and $200,000 for the Kerr Dam lease. Tribal assets were counted as $1,065,000, nearly half of which came from the tribal hot springs enterprise.[41]

The BIA further reported that the major problem concerning termination would be to organize and liquidate the tribal holdings. Although the withdrawal bills did not call for liquidation, in actuality that would be the result because of a high number of withdrawing members. The BIA admitted that there was some question about the ability of the state and local governments to pay the cost of present services from local taxes. Termination would therefore present a financial problem to the state and local governments. The BIA acknowledged that the tribes had expressed concern about the possible loss of exclusive hunting and fishing rights and about possible discrimination by non-Indians, especially in state courts. However, the BIA representatives argued that some sort of a change was necessary because the Indian Reorganization Act had not proved adequate in managing tribal assets equally.[42]

As the BIA representatives, such as D'Arcy McNickle, and congressmen, such as Wesley D'Ewart, had visited the Flathead Reservation after the war, the Salish Kootenai tribal leaders were well aware of the upcoming termination legislation. At the time of the McNickle and D'Ewart visits in 1946-1947, the tribes had not wanted to make any preparations for a possible withdrawal and the issue did not reappear until 1952. This time the tribes could not avoid the issue. Termination was not a matter people wanted to talk about, so the council hesitated to bring the issue up for tribal discussion, but ultimately it had no choice.[43] The tribal council did not address the withdrawal of federal supervision; it thought that the matter meant liquidation of tribal assets. Taxation and treaty rights provided the key points in the council's unanimous opposition to termination at Flathead. The tribes held that their lands should not be taxed because tax exemption was a privilege provided by the treaty. They concluded that they had made much progress under the IRA and argued that the termination bill did not provide adequate protection for the interests of the tribes and their members.[44] Tribal elder John Peter Paul confirmed that treaty rights and taxation were the key issues in tribal opposition to termination. The treaty of 1855 had promised the land to the tribes and withdrawing government supervision would have broken the treaty and opened the land for grabs. Many people could not afford to pay taxes on their land and would lose it. Termination would only bring hardship to tribal members, he recalled.[45]

Commissioner Myer was deeply involved early in the Flathead termination debate, but very soon disappeared from the picture. When tribal member Zephyr Gardipe wished to sell his interest in the tribe, Myer replied that any withdrawal should be by mutual agreement with the tribes.[46] The commissioner visited the reservation in August 1952 to consult with tribal representatives on the matter. At that time Myer admitted that the BIA had no specific plans on withdrawing federal services. He repeated his promise that no action would be taken without full consultation with the tribe. However, his visit of two hours comprised all of his personal contact with the tribe. If this meant full consultation, he had a different idea of the term than the tribes did. Council member Nick Lassaw did not believe this brief visit was enough.[47]

In his remarks to the council, Myer stated that the BIA was not "interested in breaking agreements or treaties" made between tribes and the federal government but alternatives should be explored to find out if there was a more effective way to provide services. He did not wish to talk about complete liquidation of federal guardianship. Myer added that the BIA did not favor encouraging Indians to live on reservations because these areas without sufficient resources could not sustain a sizable population. He urged the tribes to consider relocation of those members who did not have a way to earn a living from the land. He believed that appropriations should be continued and recommended that Indian land should not be divided. What form the reservation management would take would be left to the tribes concerned. Myer argued that the bureau could not help tribes if tribal members could not work together. The commissioner expected that the tribes would have some kind of an answer to withdrawal proposition by the end of the year so that the most significant problems could be addressed in the legislation. Myer concluded his remarks with a clear threat: "If the tribe did not come up with some answers, some one else would."[48]

Chairman Walter McDonald replied that he doubted whether the tribal council could assume all responsibilities for reservation management because of the adverse sentiments toward it from some tribal members. Commissioner Myer concurred with the chairman. He doubted that the council could take care of both administration and business thereby hinting at the possibility of a tribal corporation to manage assets.[49] McDonald later doubted that a corporation could work because there was too much jealousy towards the tribal council.[50] The Confederated Salish and Kootenai Tribes, prompted by Myer's admonition, made a concerted effort to work together. They also made sure that the State of Montana and Montana congressmen knew of their opinion. They pushed for cooperation with state officials, although not always with great success. The tribes also chose delegates to visit other reservations in order to gather information on withdrawal.[51]

After Myer's visit, it had become obvious that a Flathead termination bill would be introduced in Congress and that the tribes would have to come up with some kind of a self-management plan. Such a plan would help the tribes be prepared for their own liquidation if the termination bill should pass. Council member William Morigeau did not think that the tribes should come forward with a plan for withdrawal, but instead should present a rehabilitation program to the Indian office. He admitted that a third of the tribal enrollment was composed of members who lived off the reservation and who would probably be in favor of liquidation.[52] Louie DeMers of Arlee said that it had become essential that a self-management plan be devised. He thought that the tribes should buy Salish and Kootenai lands in heirship status. If they did not, local whites would seize the opportunity to buy additional pieces of land on the reservation.[53] Not that the tribes had not tried to buy heirship lands. In September of 1952 the tribal council requested an allocation of $100,000 from local and treasury funds for the purchase of the 190 1920 allotments located within the reservation for consolidation of tribal land holdings and to provide for the sustained production and conservation of timber resources. The purchase could not be completed due to lack of funds.[54] Paul Fickinger, BIA director for the Billings area, to which the Flathead Reservation belonged, admitted that the problem of administering these largely forested lands allotted to individuals represented a constant source of trouble. Although allotments were made to individuals, the timber had been reserved to the tribe.[55] Lack of funds also forced the clinic at St. Ignatius to close.[56]

The confederated tribes had to work with Fickinger to get the termination bill least harmful for them. Initially this relationship certainly did not look promising. In a November 1952 speech to western Indian tribes in Billings, Fickinger claimed that Indians only a few weeks earlier "were asking and agitating" for the abolition of the BIA and now they were opposing withdrawal. Fickinger used Thomas Jefferson's words of 1805, which Congressman Wesley D'Ewart had also found so quotable: "Let their settlements and ours blend together, — to intermix and become one people." Fickinger argued that the Indian Service's task had always been assimilation. Finally he showed his inexplicable ignorance by claiming that Indians did not pay taxes.[57] These comments obviously raised unfavorable feelings on the Flathead Reservation.

Forrest Stone, the Superintendent of the Flathead Reservation, reviewed with the tribal council his discussions with Commissioner Myer regarding the contents of the upcoming Flathead withdrawal bill. Stone reaffirmed that the people would be consulted on the bill. There were six topics to be considered in preparation for the withdrawal: the final tribal roll, the withdrawal of federal supervision, the withdrawal of trust status on property, the repeal of the Indian Reorganization Act, the transfer of the irrigation district to the Water-Users Association, and the termination of all Indian Bureau services. Myer had proposed two years preparation time before withdrawal would take effect.[58]

In October 1953 the tribal council went carefully with Fickinger through all the twenty sections of the first draft of H.R. 7319, the freshly introduced Flathead termination bill. The tribal council members strongly objected to the provision that essentially would make the tribes pay for their own liquidation. Fickinger stated that the Salish and Kootenai would be requested to take more responsibility regardless of whether the bill passed. The council members thought that the bill would break the treaty of 1855, but Fickinger was not so sure. Chairman Walter McDonald believed that the people on the reservation had been self-supporting thanks to the Indian Reorganization Act, which should not be nullified. He suggested that there were tribal members who were not interested in the reservation because they had lost their allotments and now favored liquidation of tribal assets for cash. McDonald thought that these members should be released on a voluntary basis, but that the rest should continue as before. Area Director Fickinger concluded that some action by the tribes to find solutions would be necessary, but stated that any or no action by Congress could be possible. He argued that many tribal members had individually or in groups requested to be freed from supervision, which had resulted in the bill.[59] According to Fickinger, the Flathead Reservation had been chosen to be liquidated because the tribes were one of the most advanced and progressive. But the proposal to terminate and the recent cuts in tribal programs revealed a gaping hole in the rhetoric; the revolving credit program had been allegedly discontinued because the tribes were poor managers, yet it would be managing the entire reservation as a corporation once termination were completed.[60]

Tribal rolls remained one of the most significant problems in the termination matter. The withdrawal bill stated that rolls would be closed on the day that withdrawal took effect. The tribes thus had to get the current rolls corrected before the secretary of the interior would decide individual tribal membership. Chairman McDonald admitted that there were 144 questionable names on the current roll.[61]

The tribal council members understood that it was necessary to present both sides of the question. There were many difficult things to consider before any final decision should be made: the special situation of the full-bloods, the irrigation problem, the incorporation of the tribes under the state and consequent taxes, individual taxation, and the possibility of selling the tribal assets. Therefore the tribes would need an extension of time for research and data collection. State and federal representatives should be invited to consult.[62]

The Salish and Kootenai had to ponder the withdrawal bill's chances for success and whether they should respond to it or not. The tribes could not come to a clear resolution of this issue. Pend d'Oreille elder Nick Lassaw suggested that if Congress passed the bill, "somebody is going to be sorry." The Wheeler-Howard Act would be repealed, and "what is there left for us?"[63] Eneas Conko believed that those favoring ending the federal supervision were making a big mistake. He wanted the tribes to have ten years to think about the issue under the status quo.[64] A meeting with local whites clarified that whites did not want the responsibility of tribal affairs. Some residents wondered about the sudden and unusual rush to push this legislation.[65]

George M. Tunison, an Iowa-born Omaha, Nebraska, attorney, had a contract with the tribes since 1941. He also represented the Shoshones of the Wind River Reservation in Wyoming. Tunison urged the development of some kind of a plan which would include provisions for withdrawal for those who so wished so that they would have an alternative to present to the BIA. He believed that the tribes would not be able to operate as a corporation because of taxation and argued that Congress would understand this point if it were explained clearly enough. The only alternative bill presented so far had been prepared by those favoring liquidation. Chairman McDonald noted that the full-bloods were backing the council and wondered about the 101 off-reservation members who had petitioned the BIA area director for the bill. Montana's senior Senator James Murray had promised to oppose the bill in Congress if the tribes so wished. Montana's other congressmen could not be reached at that time.[66] Full-bloods in general opposed any change in the present situation and wanted to be left alone. Many of them could not understand what was going on.[67]

After World War II attorneys played an important role in helping many Indian tribes deal with legal matters. Many Salish and Kootenai claim that having access to an attorney would have prevented allotment of the Flathead Reservation.[68] Certainly George Tunison's effectiveness as tribal attorney helped prevent termination of the Flathead Reservation. As was the case in many tribes, the Salish and Kootenai had claims against the United States based on the BIA's mismanagement of tribal funds and the lands ceded in the 1855 treaty. Before the founding of the Indian Claims Commission (ICC), tribal claims had to go to the U.S. Court of Claims granted that Congress approved. In 1941 Senator James Murray introduced a claims bill for the

Salish and Kootenai tribes in the Senate and Representative Jeannette Rankin, Republican from Montana, joined in the House.[69] In January 1951 the Court of Claims awarded the Salish and Kootenai tribes $550,000 for the BIA mismanagement of tribal funds. At the time of termination hearings, the tribes had a pending claim in the Indian Claims Commission concerning the 12 million acres ceded in the treaty.[70]

Pending tribal claims in the ICC may have caused some congressmen to push termination in order to avoid similar cases in the future. Senator Watkins provided a prime example of this type of thinking. He declared that it "is a good argument for getting us out of this as quick as we can, before we get some more tribes suing us."[71] After Tunison's death in July 1954, the Washington D.C. law firm of Wilkinson, Cragun, and Barker pushed the Flathead land claims to a successful conclusion in the ICC. In 1967 the tribes received an award of $4.7 million excluding attorney fees and offsets for the goods received.[72] Wilkinson, Cragun, and Barker also acted as legal counsels for the NCAI, beginning in 1953.[73]

Before the congressional hearings, the tribal council contacted all the state offices to clarify the issues at stake. The Montana Welfare Department argued that the burden on the state and counties would not increase much because the taxation of Indian land would bring in enough revenue to pay for the increased welfare costs. The tribal council, however, wanted the department to consider the next generation which would be born landless.[74] Henry Hendrickson, Lake County Commissioner, contended that counties concerned would be under a heavy financial burden for at least five years. He objected to the bill in its present form because there was no protection for the old Indians who were not able to compete on an equal basis.[75] The tribes also invited many state representatives to testify in the hearings.

Many tribal members, particularly among those living off the reservation, were more interested in short-time gain of liquidation payments instead of the relatively small annual per capita payments. The inflated estimates of the value of the Kerr Dam as $30 million and tribal lands as $40 million made liquidation seem attractive indeed.[76] Those prices would give $17,000 to each tribal member. Noel Pichette testified that he was personally attracted to "a big pile of money." Living simply from day to day made the option attractive. But he realized that the money would not have lasted. Pichette recalled that many who were uneducated thought that money would solve everything and did not realize that they would lose their relationship with the tribe.[77]

Some tribal members who did not oppose the termination bills wrote to Senator Mike Mansfield claiming that there were 750 tribal members living away from the reservation who were greatly interested in separating from the tribe. They were making a better living than those on the reservation and felt that the tribal council had nothing to offer: "the only ones who get any special monies from Tribal Council are some members of the Tribal Council and the very few employed as clerks and office help." These tribal members complained that those "very few Indians" opposing liquidation feared taxation and felt that tribal delegation opposing liquidation was unfair to a very large number of members.[78] Others thought that the only solution of fairness for all tribal members was to dispose of all tribal assets, except the power sites.[79] One tribal member believed that many had advanced through their own efforts and were capable, and he was willing to fulfill his obligations as a United States citizen. He was sure he could deal with an individual swindler better than with the BIA and wanted all tribal members, not just those living on the reservation, to have a voice in settling the question.[80]

The Senate and House Subcommittees on Indian Affairs held highly unusual joint hearings over the termination bills affecting the Flathead Reservation and other Indian communities. Congress adopted this arrangement in order to expedite the process in case Republicans lost their majority in Congress or President Dwight D. Eisenhower lost the elections of 1952.[81] Representative E. Y. Berry argued that this arrangement was made to "save taxpayers' money by not needing to bring witnesses to two hearings."[82] Chairmen Watkins and Berry agreed on the direction of the policy. Watkins set the hearings on the termination of Utah tribes first just to show that he did not pick on other states. Notification of the hearings came late to the tribes and many had a hard time sending delegates to Washington.

The hearings followed a similar pattern. In his opening statement Assistant Secretary of the Interior Orme Lewis emphasized that the level of resources, education, integration, relocation needs, state and local attitudes and, as a key, Indian attitudes had been taken into account in writing these bills. Lewis argued that generally speaking Indians were ready for the adoption of some such type of legislation. The time element would vary between the different tribes. The solicitor of the Department of the Interior had no doubt that Congress had the power to terminate federal supervision and control over Indian property.[83]

The Flathead hearings were held in February 1954. Assistant Secretary Lewis, repeating the earlier BIA report on the Flathead, admitted that tribal members residing on the reservation were decidedly against termination. However, off-reservation tribal members had generally indicated that they favored the proposed bill.[84] In fact only a handful of off-reservation tribal members had ever stated their opinion on the bill. The State of Montana Bureau of Indian Affairs had concluded that the older people in the reservation wanted security by government trust and the younger people wanted security through integration and opportunity.[85]

The most well-known tribal member, D'Arcy McNickle, testified for the tribes without an official mandate. He voiced his opposition to termination. He considered the bills hasty and ill-advised old-time assimilationist thinking. McNickle strongly urged an agreement between the tribes and the government over the termination plan. He perceived that the tribes would have to divide up their assets: "the pressure to get that divided up is going to be awfully great, on the part of people who tomorrow, after they get it, may regret that kind of solution. And it is very difficult, under this legislation, this proposed legislation, to get any other kind of result."[86] McNickle recommended that the responsibility for management ought to be transferred to the tribal governing body, which could be reorganized under state law. In the end, McNickle emphasized that the tribes should have a free choice of what to do. He argued that the tribal members living on the reservation should be the only ones to decide about who should be included in the tribal rolls and about the liquidation of tribal property, as the tribal constitution limited voting to tribal members residing in the reservation. This fact prompted Senator Watkins and Congressmen Berry and D'Ewart to declare the Salish Kootenai constitution as illegal, un-American, and putting an additional penalty on those who had left the reservation.[87]

The tribal delegates, supported by their attorney George Tunison, questioned the entire need of this legislation at that time. Tunison did not object to termination if land would not go on the tax roll. To Senator Watkins' insistence that Indians did not pay taxes, the attorney pointed out that the three tribes had furnished millions of acres of land in exchange for the tax exemption. Still Watkins claimed that the "modern conditions" had long since changed the treaty conditions. Tunison agreed with McNickle that the on-reservation tribal population should have a decisive voice over the matter and called the Indian Bureau estimate of $70 million as the net worth of tribal assets ludicrous.[88]

The Salish and Kootenai tribes sent chairman Walter McDonald, vice-chairman Walter Morigeau, land clerk Russell Gardipe, and tribal member and former chairman Steve DeMers as their delegates to the hearings. They stated that the $70 million estimate, based on overestimated timber values, had caused numerous petitions for enrollment from those willing to cash in on tribal membership. They did not argue against a reasonable bill towards ultimate withdrawal, conceding such a course of action as inevitable. But at that time they contended that the effects on tribal welfare, assets, and rights would be tragic. Chairman McDonald and his associates said that before termination could take effect, several minimum requirements should be fulfilled: Any agreement should be bilateral, with no threat of coercion; all claims should be settled; the federal government should assist in negotiations with the state and county governments; a complete survey and inventory of resources was needed; a minimum of ten years of planning should be required and both parties should have access to the U.S. Court of Appeals. Tribal delegates would accept federal withdrawal if tribal land remained in tax exempt status. They realized that corporation taxes of up to fifty percent would be too high to enable the tribes to pay their administrative and other expenses. Vice-Chairman Morigeau worried about timber resources: "If we were to be liquidated, and the land was taxable — I don't think it should be broken up. We probably would be forced to sell that land in strips, timber and land. That is a national resource."[89]

Land clerk Gardipe pointed out that the government policy of issuing fee patents had led to loss of land. He feared that termination would lead to similar results. Chairman McDonald noted that tribal members could not compete on farming because of lack of credit, thereby pointing out the ultimate contradiction of the termination policy: Congress and the BIA argued that the tribes were progressive and advanced but had cut off their loan program because they were poor managers. Tribal leaders particularly worried about the welfare of the less acculturated full-bloods and the elderly.[90] The most important issue to the tribes remained the treaty of 1855 and tribal rights based on it. Termination threatened these rights.[91]

Senator Watkins treated tribal delegates with disrespect as they did not fulfill his view of a "real Indian." He scorned them for not being more than half-bloods and claimed that the Salish Kootenai tribes treated their full-bloods poorly because Kootenai Jerome Hewankorn was the only full-blood in the tribal council. After stating that he had "lived in a reservation once, and I know how those things go," Watkins showed his ignorance of tribal traditions and history by concluding that the full-bloods must have made a mistake in the past by adopting whites and Indians of low tribal blood as tribal members. He also could not understand why the tribes would not approve something that was "for your good."[92] To Watkins' insistence on allowing all tribal members to vote, Vice-Chairman Walter Morigeau noted that the trouble in that was that those living on the reservation own property there and would have that property at stake in the referendum. Those living on the reservation depended on tribal land to operate cattle ranches or farms and would lose their livelihood should tribal lands be sold due to liquidation. At this point Congressman D'Ewart concurred with Morigeau, realising the drastic effects to the tribal timber and cattle resources should the bills be passed as written.[93]

Paul Charlo testified with the help of an interpreter. He wanted more time for termination plans so that the younger generation could be able to take care of him and the other elderly. Jerome Hewankorn, a full-blood Kootenai councilman, testified against the claim that Indians did not pay taxes. He admitted that the tribal property was tax exempt, but Indians paid all sales taxes.[94] Born in 1892, Hewankorn lived in the Kootenai community of Dayton in the northern end of the reservation. He owned 300 acres of land, most of it for grazing as he had 23 head of livestock and nine horses. He also farmed 90 acres, which provided most of his cash income.[95]

Those favoring termination also had their representatives in the hearings. Lorena Burgess received support from Annastasia

Jerome Hewankorn, (center), Kootenai member of the
Confederated Salish and Kootenai Tribes Tribal Council.
Representative Lee Metcalf, Senator James E. Murray, Senator
Mike Mansfield, and Representative LeRoy Anderson (left to
right) in Murray's office in the 1950s.

Source: Mike Mansfield Papers MSS 065, photograph 99-2314, Archives
and Special Collections, Mansfield Library, University of Montana,
Missoula, Montana.

Wievoda, Vera Voorhies, and Lulu Charrier. They argued, without evidence, that they represented the wishes of the majority of the tribes in wanting liquidation of the reservation. Such action would give the members complete control of their own affairs. They labeled the tribal government based on the Indian Reorganization Act as socialistic. They complained that the recent per capita payments by the tribal council had been unfairly low and illegal. These individuals particularly complained about the rolls of 1908 and 1920; many Indians were then dropped from the tribal rolls. At the same time, they also wanted to make sure that safeguards on tribal rights, care of the elderly, and education would be maintained.[96]

This pro-terminationist group had prepared its own version of a termination bill. It had also circulated petitions for liquidation asking individuals to sign. Chairman McDonald did not want the tribal council to have any responsibility for these petitions, which, he argued, were a risk for misunderstanding and misrepresentation.[97] Vera Voorhies urged for liquidation because, she argued, the highly paid attorney wanted to keep tribe as wards, assets were not being used, the Wheeler-Howard Act should be repealed, and a true tribal roll should be determined. Voorhies had tried to exchange her 160 acres allotment for 68 acres of tribal land, but neither the tribal council nor the BIA had approved the exchange because her allotment was less valuable than the 68 acres she wanted.[98]

Senator Arthur Watkins repeated throughout the hearings his views that the basic reason why Indians opposed termination stemmed from their desire to avoid their fair share of taxation. He declared: "we all must realize that we have responsibilities to help pay for the things that we actually use." Watkins argued that any Indian with less than half Indian blood was actually white and only pretended to be an Indian to have privileges.[99] Treaties had established the pattern of tribal trust land, but to Watkins treaties could be easily discarded given congressional plenary power which did not require Indian consent. He simply ignored treaty rights and considered any new information that contradicted his position as irrelevant. Watkins treated anyone who dared to oppose his perspective with arrogance and contempt. He believed that his ideas represented fairness for all Americans, but failed to realize that the assimilation of Native Americans would and could not happen overnight. To him rhetoric seemed to be more important than careful study; no anthropologists nor historians were invited to present testimony at the hearings. In order to obtain congressional support, the subcommittees carefully used language that presented the policy as beneficial to the tribes and de-emphasized the cuts in administrative costs.[100]

The Flathead termination bill was defeated after the February 1954 hearings. Watkins reintroduced the bill in June 1954, but Senator James Murray held it in the committee and it never came up for a second hearing.[101] Although clearly divided, the Salish and Kootenai appeared strong in their opposition to termination. The majority of tribal people opposed termination of their reservation fearing it would result in hardship and loss of land just like the removal from the Bitterroots and allotment had done. Both events were still fresh in the people's memory. Noel Pichette saw termination as a continuum — a part of historical legacy starting with the Jesuits who took Salish religion and language away. White prejudice against Indians contributed to this legacy.[102] The unanimous opposition of the tribal council proved decisive. The defeat of termination came with a price: It meant the alienation of a significant number of tribal members particularly among those living off the reservation. This alienation showed in the renewed termination effort of the early 1970s. The tribes had been progressive and adapted to the white culture around them, but they appeared unprepared to manage effectively their assets without government supervision. Most importantly, the tribes convinced the Montana state officials and Montana's congressional delegation that termination would have only ill effects in the region. Strong opposition assured the committee members that termination of the Flathead Reservation would not succeed. This was in contrast with the Utes of the Uintah-Ouray Reservation in Utah, the Wisconsin Menominees, and the Klamath in Oregon. Effective opposition was missing against the termination of these reservations, opening the door to the success of the policy.

Walter McDonald and his nephew, Joseph McDonald, at Angus
McDonald's gravestone, middle 1970s.

Source: Preston Miller Collection, Four Winds Indian Trading Post,
St. Ignatius, Montana.

Walter McDonald and bagpipe, middle 1970s.

Source: Preston Miller Collection, Four Winds Indian Trading Post,
St. Ignatius, Montana.

Chapter 3

Tribal, State, and Congressional Factors in Termination: A Comparison Between Flathead and Three Terminated Reservations

Tribal and Indian affairs organizations combined to oppose termination, but that alliance was not enough to defeat the legislation. Ultimately the fate of any Indian community rested on the actions of the representatives of a particular state in the United States Congress and on state officials. The Salish and Kootenai tribes succeeded in gaining the support of the State of Montana and its congressional representatives. Without this support, the termination attempt at Flathead might have ended differently. This chapter deals with the views of the four men who represented Montana in Washington, D.C.: Senators James Murray and Mike Mansfield and Representatives Wesley D'Ewart and Lee Metcalf. Three of these four voiced their opposition to termination, and their voices were significant. The state and county governments in Montana largely feared the possible negative consequences of the withdrawal of federal supervision, especially increased costs in welfare and administration, which the added tax base could not cover. This opinion proved decisive, as one of the prerequisites for termination was the capability and willingness of the state to assume the federal responsibilities. Unlike their Montana counterparts, Wisconsin, Oregon, and Utah officials were non-committal in regard to termination and did not oppose it with the same degree of intensity. In addition, the Klamath, Menominee, and Utah Ute tribes were more factionalized than the Salish-Kootenai. Given these circumstances, it is perhaps not surprising that these groups were terminated.

Republican Representative Wesley D'Ewart favored withdrawal of at least some federal supervision from Indian affairs. First elected to the House of Representatives in 1945, he was re-elected four times and lost his seat after an unsuccessful campaign to defeat Senator James Murray in the 1954 elections. That campaign showed D'Ewart's avowed ideology of anti-Communism, as he attacked Senator Murray as a tool of Communist infiltration through a questionable publication titled "Red Web over Congress." After D'Ewart's fall from Congress, President Dwight D. Eisenhower's Secretary of the Interior, Douglas McKay, offered him a position in the cabinet, first as an assistant to the Secretary of Agriculture, and then as Assistant Secretary of the Interior in 1955. The Senate Interior Committee, influenced by Senator Murray, refused to confirm the latter nomination due to the ugly campaign of 1954 and because of D'Ewart's record in Congress. In Congress he had promoted mining, grazing, and lumber interests at the expense of Native Americans and the environment, which raised opposition from many circles.[1]

In September 1945, D'Ewart introduced a bill to "provide for removal of restrictions on property of Indians who serve in the armed forces." This bill represented one of the first proposals relating to termination. It drew heavy criticism in D'Ewart's home state. Luella Johnk of Billings saw the bill as an "opening wedge to take from the Indian what little he has left." She believed that with less bureaucratic control and tax-free land many Indians could make a better living on the reservation than off it. Suggesting that D'Ewart's true interests in the matter lay elsewhere, Johnk asked: "How much bonus will you get from the various live stock interests and real estate associations?"[2] Another Montana critic, anthropologist Carling Malouf of the University of Montana, Missoula, believed that D'Ewart's connections to cattle interests "may or may not have some bearing on the matter" of the Flathead Reservation having been chosen for termination. Malouf had no doubt that the neighboring whites would greatly benefit at the expense of Indians due to tax foreclosures were the reservation terminated.[3]

In 1951 and 1952 D'Ewart had introduced bills to confer jurisdiction of Indian reservations to states. A Montana Supreme Court ruling that the state had no jurisdiction on the reservation except in the case of a major crime prompted D'Ewart's action.[4] These bills had formed a precedent for Public Law 280 of 1953. That same year, D'Ewart joined a special investigative subcommittee of the House Interior and Insular Affairs Committee on a visit to the Flathead agency to hear Indian testimony for and against the withdrawal of federal supervision. Chairman William H. Harrison declared that the intent of Congress was not to force any "unreasonable conditions upon the Indians."[5] A number of enrolled members of the Salish and Kootenai tribes, including Vera Voorhies, Lorena Burgess, and Anna Weivoda, thanked Representative Harrison for this visit and urged orderly liquidation of the reservation.[6]

In the termination hearings D'Ewart, a member of the House Indian Affairs Subcommittee, cautiously expressed his views that the withdrawal of federal supervision should take place at Flathead and should not require approval of the on-reservation tribal members. He had read, and possibly approved in advance, Lorena Burgess' statement for termination and believed that it was excellent.[7] After the hearings, D'Ewart repeated his conviction that certain functions of the Indian Bureau, particularly education, should be turned over to state and county control. Indians should be given the right to assume competency if they so wished. D'Ewart wanted to continue negotiating with the Salish and Kootenai to analyze what would be needed to assume their roles as individual citizens and taxpayers.[8]

Born on a farm near St. Thomas, Ontario, Canada, in 1876, James Murray was a son of Irish immigrants. He moved to

Senator James Murray

Source: Photograph 81-10, Archives and Special Collections, Mansfield
Library, University of Montana, Missoula, Montana.

Butte, Montana, in his twenties and made a fortune in business ventures. Trained as a lawyer, Murray first gained election to the United States Senate in 1934 on the coattails of President Franklin D. Roosevelt. According to his biographer, Donald Spritzer, Murray remained a New Dealer long after the death of the New Deal. Murray, Spritzer suggested, had a "strongly felt sense of 'noblesse oblige,' a belief that those well off were responsible for the welfare of people less fortunate." Like most New Dealers, Murray looked to the federal government as the only agent large and powerful enough to prevent exploitation of the majority by the bankers and organized forces of monopoly.[9] No wonder, then, that in the 1950's Murray's views came under scrutiny by the anti-Communist warriors of McCarthyism.

Murray was particularly interested in domestic affairs. Of Montana's congressional delegation, he reacted most actively to the Indian legislation. By the 1950's, his senior position in the Senate gave him additional influence. Murray had supported Montana's senior Senator Burton Wheeler's bill to repeal the Indian Reorganization Act in 1937. At that time, Murray considered the act a detriment to Indian tribal structure.[10] After Republicans gained a majority in Congress in 1947, they started to cut New Deal programs. Indian affairs constituted one of the targets. Officials of Montana school districts with large Indian enrollments worried about these cuts as they needed supplemental appropriations because Indian lands were largely tax-exempt. Senator Murray promised to try and restore funds for Montana school districts.[11] Wavering like a true politician, Murray at the same time believed that reductions, or elimination, of BIA appropriations could be considered.[12]

Murray argued that the president should appoint unprejudiced people to study and make recommendations on Indian affairs because Interior Department studies were innately biased.[13] In early 1950, Murray wrote that the answer to the Indian relief problem lay in the formulation of long-range plans for permanent work and rehabilitation programs on the reservation.[14] The senator concluded, perhaps mistakenly, that eventual withdrawal of government supervision was inevitable. Therefore he was determined to prepare the Indians for this eventuality by increasing their educational and technical assistance. The National Congress of American Indians (NCAI) and other tribal representatives had all along been urging such support as an alternative to relocation.

Prompted by the NCAI, Murray introduced Senate Concurrent Resolution 85 in July 1956 and Senate Concurrent Resolution 3 in January 1957. These were patterned after the American Point Four Programs, which gave technical and educational aid to underdeveloped areas of the world. Similar measures should be applied in Indian reservations, Murray, NCAI, and many others believed.[15] The Salish Kootenai tribal chairman Walter McDonald, the State of Montana, and Senator Mike Mansfield supported these bills. For once Murray agreed with Senator William Langer, one of the congressional terminationists, by arguing that relocation did not solve the problem of reservation poverty and Indian slums around urban centers. The resolutions would have nullified HCR 108 and encouraged the initiative and consent of Indian people in promoting their welfare.[16] These proposals did not gain adequate backing. Prompted by Secretary of the Interior Fred Seaton's speech of 1958, Murray introduced Senate Concurrent Resolution 12 in 1959 to interpret HCR 108 as stating an objective, not an immediate goal. Congressman Metcalf introduced parallel HCR 92 in the House.[17]

In the Flathead termination hearings the Montana senators cooperated. Either Murray or Mansfield sat through the proceedings, watching and making sure that tribal views got a fair hearing. They pointed out the probable negative consequences of the bills. Murray particularly feared that the tribes would not be able to bid on the Kerr Dam if the tribal assets were disposed. The tribes would therefore lose their largest income. Murray argued that Indians should have a right to vote on whether they wanted this legislation or not.[18] The flaws in the 1954 termination bills were, as Murray saw it, that they disregarded the wishes of the Indians and ignored the illiteracy and unpreparedness of members of some tribes to make a living in competition with other Americans.[19] Murray believed that, as written, the Flathead termination bills (S. 2750 and H.R. 7319) would not benefit the tribe. This was the key to his opposition. Nevertheless, he admitted: "we all recognize that the Government's responsibility over the Indians must be terminated at some time." But the bills provided too little time for this to happen.[20] Senator Mansfield was aware that the termination bills would violate the treaty of 1855. He wanted assurances that this would not eventually happen, but Rex Lee, the Associate Commissioner of Indian Affairs, could not give such assurances. Mansfield wanted to make sure that all tribal representatives who had arrived from Montana could get their voices heard through testimony.[21] Representative Lee Metcalf could not personally appear in the hearings, but he had a lengthy statement on state and county officials' views printed in the record.

Senator Murray worked hard to come to terms with the issue of withdrawal and the extent of federal services to Indians. He admitted that Indians should not always receive special services from the government. He only wanted to make sure that withdrawal would not happen before Indians and their communities could survive on the same level as their non-Indian neighbors. That is why he complained about the BIA's land and credit policy. Commissioner Glenn Emmons wanted Indians to obtain loans from the private market, which is why one half of the money available for loans to Indians sat idle in the U.S. Treasury. Murray felt that this policy was leading to rapid indebtedness of Indian communities.[22]

Murray served on the Senate Committee on Interior and Insular Affairs from 1948 until his retirement in 1961. From

1955 Murray chaired this committee, a position he gained after Senator Hugh Butler's death. From this post he had a chance to block further attempts at termination. In 1958 Murray led an inquiry into the growing loss of tribal lands through sale. Tribal people had expressed their apprehension in numerous letters to the senator and in the newsletters of Indian interest groups. Murray argued that Commissioner Emmons' policy to allow sales of Indian lands decreased the Indian land base, which in turn seriously impaired the effective use of tribal and individual trust land as economic units. While the committee questionnaire was being answered in the agencies and tribal organizations, Murray asked the secretary of the interior to declare a moratorium on Indian land sales, a request to which the secretary yielded. The greatest land losses had taken place in the jurisdiction of the Billings, Montana, area office, where over one million acres of individual Indian trust land had been sold.[23]

Michael J. or "Mike" Mansfield was born in 1903 and was raised in Great Falls, Montana. Before his election to the United States Congress in 1943, Mansfield taught Latin American and Far Eastern history in the University of Montana, Missoula. After ten years in the House, Mansfield was elected to the Senate in 1953. Foreign affairs remained his primary interest; Mansfield gained a seat on the prestigious Senate Foreign Relations Committee as a freshman. Few first year senators gained such an assignment. Mansfield became one of the foreign policy experts in the Senate and served as the majority leader from 1961 until his retirement in 1977. After retirement from Congress, Mansfield served as United States ambassador to Japan.[24]

Mansfield agreed with Murray that eventually the federal government would relinquish all responsibility to Indians. Both of them disagreed with the likes of Senator Watkins about the timing of termination. Mansfield wanted an adequate time period for preparation and the consent of the governed. He believed that education would provide the answer to many of the

Senator Mike Mansfield

Source: Photograph 85-212, Archives and Special Collections, Mansfield Library, University of Montana, Missoula, Montana.

problems Indians faced. Indians could enter American society as equals, but assimilation had to happen with restraint and careful execution.[25]

Senator Mansfield felt that Commissioner Emmons and the Interior Department officials eagerly promoted relocation and movement off the reservation knowing full well that Indians, once removed from the reservation, would no longer be eligible for federal aid. To make the relocation program successful, Indians should be better prepared for what to expect through an educational program at the community level. At the same time, BIA policies left Indian reservations in a deplorable condition.[26] Mansfield warned that the historical responsibility of the federal government could not be discarded lightly. All Indians should be the responsibility of the federal government regardless of tribal affiliation or location.[27] Mansfield suggested that to have success in improving reservation conditions, Indians had to help themselves with the assistance and guidance of the various federal agencies. Substantial loan funds should be made available for this purpose.[28]

Lee Metcalf hailed from the Bitterroot River Valley community of Stevensville, named after Isaac Stevens, the governor of Washington Territory, who signed the treaty with the Salish and Kootenai bands in 1855. Fort Owen and St. Mary's Mission were located in Stevensville. Metcalf was born in 1911, twenty years after the last Salish were removed from the area to the reservation further north. He earned a law degree at University of Montana, Missoula, in 1936. Metcalf served on the Montana Supreme Court before his election to Congress to succeed Mansfield in the House of Representatives. When Senator Murray retired in 1961, Metcalf followed him in the Senate, where he served until his death in 1978.[29]

Metcalf quickly established himself in Indian affairs by opposing withdrawal of federal supervision unless the tribal council and the members of the tribes agreed on the legislation. He thus

Representative Lee Metcalf at 42 years old, about 1953.

Source: DeWalt Studio and Camera Shop, Helena, Montana, photographer,
Lot 31 B1/5.05, Photographic Archives, Montana, Historical Society,
Helena, Montana.

Representative Lee Metcalf, wearing Native American headdress, dancing with Indian dancers, about 1950s. (Indians in picture are not from the Flathead Indian Reservation.)
Source: June Moncure, Missoula, Montana, photographer, Lot 31 B6/3.07, Photographic Archives, Montana Historical Society, Helena, Montana.

emphasized the need for Indian consent to policies affecting them. He insisted that there should be some provision for continued tribal ownership of assets if that was the wish of the tribe. Timber holdings should not be sold off on a piece-meal basis but must be incorporated into some sort of a sustained-yield operation in order to protect the national forests.[30] Metcalf pointed out that while he was on the Montana Supreme Court in 1951, the court noted that the 1855 treaty was a grant of rights from the Indians, not to them, with a reservation remaining to them in exchange. Therefore he could not accept any violation of the treaty. Time was an important concern; more time was needed before the federal government could walk out from its responsibility for Indians and leave the state and local taxpayers "holding the bag."[31]

After the termination drive had slowed down, Metcalf attacked its basic terminology and the reasoning that American Indians would become "first class" citizens only if "we break the promises we made them and take away their benefits." He wrote that everybody believed that regulations should be removed and that the BIA should eventually be abolished, but this could not happen before ample preparation time and before Indians had a chance to integrate into mainstream America. Metcalf believed that some of the termination bills that passed had been accepted by the tribes concerned.[32] But, on the other hand, the BIA had used "duress, blackmail and pressure" to get Indian agreement, Metcalf charged. He predicted that next Congress would force the BIA to reverse its policy by repealing HCR 108.[33] The representative claimed that because of the sad state of Indian reservations, the deceptive slogan that the government must be out of Indian affairs appealed to uninformed outsiders.[34]

Metcalf claimed that economic interests fueled the drive for termination: "the motivation came from people who would like to get their hands on the Indians' resources." Metcalf specifically criticized Commissioner Emmons claiming that some of the commissioner's concern for the Indians' welfare was "phoney" and occasionally false. He argued that the relocation program was pushed too hard and too fast leaving most of the relocated families inadequately prepared to face urban problems. Instead of relocation, the BIA should develop an effective land program, which, coupled with a development of irrigation systems, soil and moisture conservation, and improvement of range lands, would contribute to solving reservation problems.[35] Relocation assistance should be provided to alleviate reservation poverty, but no pressure should be put on Indians to leave the reservation, Metcalf concluded.[36]

In a national television broadcast, Metcalf charged that "the country's Indian policies . . . are calculated to sandbag the Indians into selling their land and their other resources. Whether these are intentional or inadvertent, they're working for the benefit of outside pressures . . . " He mentioned the Montana Power Company and grazing operators as examples of these outside interests. The BIA itself encouraged termination in a manner that was, in effect, a forced sale. Metcalf concluded that people had never thought about the potential impact upon the welfare system that termination would have, nor had they pondered the loss of tribal identity termination would cause.[37] In a scathing 31 page response, the Department of the Interior claimed that Metcalf's statements were totally untrue and that BIA had not bullied tribes into accepting termination.[38]

In general, then, the three M's of the Montana delegation sympathized with the long-range aims of the Truman and Eisenhower administrations to "get out of the Indian business." But they emphasized that such a goal could not be achieved overnight. Donald Spritzer and Larry Hasse argued that with other congressional liberals they faced a dilemma; they found it difficult to support evident tribal segregation in special reservation trust areas while supporting integration of African-Americans. A moderate termination plan seemed to offer a way out of this dilemma by proposing for the Indians the same as the blacks were being offered: full citizenship and more equality.[39] Eventually the western liberals, typified by Senators Murray and Mansfield, formed a nucleus of opposition to termination just as eastern liberals abandoned their interest and involvement in Indian affairs.[40] They did not oppose termination rigorously until tribal opposition and the correspondence they received during the termination struggle overwhelmingly pointed to the negative effects of the policy. The Cold War hysteria and other domestic and international issues of post-war recovery occupied much of their time. Indian affairs were not very high on their priority list.

Dam projects near or on Indian land were common in the 1950's, as exemplified by the Pick-Sloan Plan on the Missouri River in the Dakotas and the Kinzua Dam on the Allegheny River in New York and Pennsylvania. Senator Murray's pet project had been the Hungry Horse Dam on the South Fork of the Flathead River northeast of the Flathead Reservation. This project was completed in 1948.[41] Over tribal protests, Senators Murray and Mansfield and Representative Metcalf supported power plants and construction of power lines on Indian reservations. They dismissed complaints of the Salish and Kootenai tribal council that some projects encroached upon their lands and violated their treaty rights. Murray saw cheap power as a key to Montana's future and Mansfield emphasized the need to bring new industries into the state.[42] The two senators supported plans to build the Knowles and Paradise Dams on the Flathead River just west of the reservation in the 1950s and 1960s. Both of these dams would have primarily flooded land on the reservation. The Salish and Kootenai tribes wanted to have a part in the development, annual payments, and an allotment of power, which the plan did not provide.[43] The tribes wanted to develop the Buffalo Rapids site within the reservation as an alternative. The Knowles Dam would have inundated this site, which is why the tribes opposed it. At a minimum, the tribes wanted considerable compensation for loss of its own site.[44]

The Salish and Kootenai tribes opposed any waterpower development off the reservation that would have impacted the value of dam sites in tribal ownership. Even dams outside the reservation that would have flooded possible sites within it would cut tribal revenues in the future if the tribes chose to develop their power resources. Dam sites were valuable tribal assets and the tribes sought the best deal. They wanted to throw the estimate of $30 million as the value of the Kerr Dam back to the government. The Knowles Dam also would have flooded 16,000 acres of tribal land and 3,000 acres of allotted land.[45] Lorena Burgess, who otherwise favored termination but lived near the possible Paradise Dam site and in the flood zone, objected to the dam because the area it would flood was set apart for the tribes' use in the 1855 treaty.[46]

County and state officials did not directly testify in the congressional hearings, but Representative Metcalf had their responses to his inquiry printed in the record. Mary Condon, State Superintendent of Public Instruction, argued that with federal help Montana had done a superb job of integrating Indian children into its public school system. Ninety percent of Indian children attended public schools. The total cost of their education was $1.5 million, of which the federal government provided $365,000. Condon argued that the problems of Indian schooling stemmed from reservations where tax exempt tribal lands furnished a limited tax base. She contended that termination would only transfer education problems entirely to state and local taxpayers as the tax revenue from Indian property would not compensate the local school districts for the loss of federal aid. Condon also argued that the termination bills were poorly planned and ill-advised. A longer transition period was needed. State and local governments had not been consulted in preparation of the bills despite their vital interest in Indian welfare.[47]

W. J. Fouse, from the State Department of Public Welfare, found it difficult to make an estimate as to the additional cost to the State Welfare Department because there were so many factors involved. The BIA Area Director argued that the revenue from taxes to be paid by Indians would cover the cost of added welfare and other expenditures on the reservation, but the tribes disagreed. Fouse said that his department would need a crystal ball to make any valid estimate. He did think that a longer transition period would decrease impacts on everyone concerned.[48] Yet elsewhere Fouse estimated that if not the state then at least the local health departments would collapse unless the local governments were able to absorb the cost of the withdrawn federal appropriations.[49]

Health care costs affected the consideration of termination. For example, tuberculosis among Indians was a problem for the State of Montana. State and county governments would not be able to carry the additional burden of financing the care of Indian patients.[50] K. W. Bergan, the State Coordinator of Indian Affairs, agreed that termination would not solve the tuberculosis problem among Indians nor other unsolved problems. The state could deal with them given money and time, but federal assistance was needed. Bergan considered relocation necessary because the state Indian population was so concentrated.[51] Replying to the governor's request on the effects of termination in the state, Bergan noted: "The general feeling is that certain impacts will fall upon the State of Montana especially in the fields of Health, Welfare and Education."[52] Bergan emphasized the importance of showing unity as Montanans against the bills: "Pattern set at this time will be extremely vital in all future withdrawal programs" for other Montana reservations.[53]

In 1952, Montana Governor John Bonner decided that there had been enough investigations of Indian affairs. He declared it was time to act. Bonner thought that the solution to many problems would come when Indians found it possible to leave the reservation. He believed that action by states offered the only hope to give Indians their rightful place in society as states had a greater interest in the Indian problem than the federal government. In keeping with this philosophy, Governor Bonner recommended to the Montana legislature that it authorize establishment of the office of Indian Coordinator. K. W. Bergan held this office.[54] Bonner's successor as governor, Hugo Aronson, having received opinions of the various state departments on the effects of termination in Montana, concluded that the ultimate aim of granting full citizenship rights and privileges to Indians represented a commendable objective. But before it could be achieved, adequate safeguards to protect the elderly full-bloods were needed, the federal government should participate financially during the transition period, and treaty rights should be fully explored.[55] While most Montana officials agreed with the principle of termination, they were divided about the method and time needed to reach that goal. Therefore it is no wonder that the state voiced its opposition to the termination bills, which proposed nearly immediate withdrawal of federal supervision.

If state officials thought that termination would cause an unbearable financial burden on the state, the four county governments having areas in the Flathead Reservation determined that there would be no additional financial burden on the counties. Indeed, according to the counties, the additional revenue realized when Indian trust lands became taxable would exceed any additional welfare and other costs. County officials emphasized that no race discrimination existed in their area.[56] As early as 1947, Lake County, Polson being the county seat, where most of the reservation population and the most valuable tribal assets were situated, could not "begin to tell the benefits our County would derive" [from Senator Butler's termination bill]. "The Indian himself will be better off if emancipated." This opinion derived from the fact that 57 percent of county lands were untaxable.[57] Jean Turnage, the Lake County Attorney and a member of the Confederated Salish and Kootenai Tribes, also urged passage or amendment of federal laws to enable state courts to assume full and complete jurisdiction on Indian reservations because the law enforcement situation in the reservations was unworkable.[58] The Lake County Democratic Committee argued that tribal council authority did not promote the maximum benefit for the whole, but benefitted council members and their administrative staff, most of whom were "of a minor degree of Indian blood." The entire Indian service loomed as a menace to local economic welfare and opportunity.[59] These opinions no doubt gave the impression that Lake County disliked the presence of a strong tribal government and seemed ready and willing to assume the responsibility for Indian affairs. On the other hand, the Montana Legislature amended the state's Public Welfare Act in 1951 to provide that counties would not be required to pay general relief to ward Indians.[60]

Numerous individual Montanans and various organizations representing different interests in the state expressed their opinions on the termination issue. These opinions overwhelmingly opposed the policy. The significance of this opposition should not be underestimated. Dennis Dellwo, secretary of the Flathead Irrigation District, which would also be terminated as a part of the termination of the Flathead Reservation, was sure that if all the property of the district — millions in value — were to be distributed to any of the Indian or non-Indian members of the district, these individuals would be "busted" within a short while.[61] Raymond Gray, a landless Indian, was certain that termination would hasten the destruction of a race of people who would become dependent and a welfare burden.[62] Emma Koliha, a Montana Chippewa, complained that if an Indian opposed the withdrawal of federal supervision he was labeled unpatriotic because he would not pay taxes on his trust land. If he said he supported it, he knew that he would lose the backing of a tribal organization and need to make it on his own. Koliha did not think Indians could make it without the federal government as whole tribes, even if some individuals would be fine.[63]

Dorothy Bohn from the Cascade County Community Council (Great Falls), a non-political body composed of delegates from civic and social-agency groups dedicated to creating an atmosphere of understanding in the community, noted the basic contradiction in the termination ideology: While the Salish and Kootenai had been given very little responsibility in the actual management of their resources before, they were now asked to take over the full management of their assets, without an adequate transition period.[64] The council was deeply concerned about the bills, which Bohn declared "a land grab," as the Flathead Reservation included timberlands, water resources, and dam sites. Other Montana reservations had rich oil and mineral resources and would therefore be the next targets.[65] While Bohn agreed that every effort should be made to assimilate the Indian in society, she insisted that it should take place without destroying his pride in his heritage and eliminating the basic pattern of his culture. She also warned that discrimination was very real in Montana.[66]

The Montana Committee Against Termination also refused to "go along with the propaganda language" of the termination program. The group offered alternatives: The consequences of termination should be studied and responsibilities fixed, attitudes of citizens in Indian states should be studied, lessons of Canada's tribally owned land and Mexico's land reforms should be learned.[67] Unfortunately this advice went largely unheeded.

The Montana Farmer's Union represented 14,000 farm families, almost one half of all the farm families in the state. Richard Shipman, a Lewistown farmer/rancher and the vice-chairman of the union, opposed the withdrawal of federal supervision because the Indians' economic future and the well-being of the entire state would be injured. The union's opposition rested on three grounds: moral, economic, and legal. The moral aspect was the most important; the treaty of 1855 would be broken if the reservation were terminated. Moreover, Shipman believed that the tribes had not been adequately consulted. The Farmer's Union anticipated that new expenses would fall in the lap of taxpayers. Shipman pointed out that the majority of Indians living on the reservation opposed withdrawal and were apprehensive about it. The State of Montana had no laws protecting Indians against discrimination. Many outsiders coveted Indian water resources and timber stands, Shipman warned. He feared that the Blackfeet, Fort Peck, and Fort Belknap reservations would be next in line as speculation for oil and other resources needed only a rumor to begin. He wondered about the hurry to withdraw, as the Salish and Kootenai had become self-supporting thanks to the present reservation framework. The termination bills provided only two options — liquidation or corporation management — but they did not allow remaining under the status quo, which the tribes preferred. Shipman warned that the tribes could not compete with large corporations to protect their resources because of economic and discriminatory reasons. As a result, they would lose these key assets.[68]

However, some Montanans believed that the Flathead Reservation should be terminated. One individual wrote to Senator Murray: "These Indians are absolutely capable of making their own way in any community." This person thought that all the opposition came from Indians owning enough property to pay taxes or from those having high-paying jobs that would disappear (obviously BIA employees).[69] Besides non-Indians living on the reservation, many Montanans living outside the borders of any of the state's seven reservations resented the "special privileges" they thought Indians had. These people would have liked to see reservations terminated and trust lands become taxable. There clearly was a serious problem of discrimination against Indians in Montana. The state and the counties concerned did not permit Indians to share in the benefits of local taxes even when they paid such taxes. This situation would continue as long as any Indian lands remained in trust status.[70]

Ronan and Polson, the largest communities in the reservation, were predominantly non-Indian. Their population was largely white and most property was in non-Indian ownership. Newspapers published in these small towns represented the views of non-Indians unhappy that tribally owned lands were tax-exempt. Editorial columns by one "H. M." in the *Flathead Courier* of Polson supported the anti-Communist views of McCarthyism and reflected western views of a pioneer spirit and intolerance towards anything considered liberal. "H. M." thought that the majority of Indians wanted "freedom," but tribal leaders held them back. The editorials also were skeptical of the usefulness of the BIA, as "Very few of the Indians can tell just what benefits they are now receiving from the federal government." Congress should protect individual Indians not tribal government's authority.[71] "H. M." argued that the elimination of the BIA, or parts of it, would be of great benefit to almost all Americans. To wait another ten years, as the Salish and Kootenai suggested, would only allow the property problems and racial situation to deteriorate further. The question of self-rule should be submitted to all tribal members, not just those on the reservation, as the tribal leaders suggested.[72] The *Ronan Pioneer* could not understand why Indians, who for years had complained about the Indian Bureau, now opposed their freedom from it. The newspaper argued that Indians, like old people, feared change, even if most would be fine after the end of federal supervision.[73] Obviously this writer ignored that some of the Indians indeed were old and fearful of the future and that some of them could not make it once federal supervision was ended.

An off-reservation Indian settlement called Hill 57 outside Great Falls worried many Montanans. Thanks to Montana welfare groups and congressmen, this settlement became a national symbol of urban Indian poverty. Unlike the landless Chippewas who were granted a reservation at Rocky Boy in 1916, the Canadian Cree, who had escaped Louis Riel's rebellion in 1885, gained no reserve of their own in Montana. Some, like D'Arcy McNickle's mother, managed to become adopted as members of other tribes. The rest became drifters, many ending up in the Great Falls area in the 1920s for seasonal work.[74] The grievances of this settlement had become well known by the early 1940s. Plans for rehabilitation had been made and Senator Murray introduced bills to give land to these landless Indians during his chairmanship of the Senate Committee on Interior and Insular Affairs. Despite Murray's efforts, no results were achieved. County officials denied welfare to these people because they considered all Indians the responsibility of the federal government. At the same time the BIA refused assistance because these Indians lived off the reservation and had never lived on one. The bureau also noted that many were Canadian citizens and some owned their homes. It concluded that these Indians presented a completely local problem. Expansion of federal responsibility to such a group appeared therefore to be out of the question.[75]

An organization called Friends of Hill 57 worked to improve the conditions of these landless. Max Gubatayao, the chairman of this organization, labeled as unrealistic the BIA's policy of adhering to state welfare standards. He also expressed alarm that the tribal council of the Salish and Kootenai tribes seemed to agree on the inevitability of termination. Gubatayao blamed the manipulation of the BIA Area Director for this stance.[76] As early as 1937, and periodically after that, some residents of Great Falls had wanted to set aside a 40-acre tract for the landless Indians of Hill 57, but either the other city residents or the BIA did not want any Indians to occupy valuable land.[77] Ironically, Montanans later believed that through implementation of termination the reservation would be liquidated, which, along with relocation, would turn the Salish and Kootenai into poor and landless like those Indians at Hill 57.[78]

Besides the Salish and Kootenai, other Montana tribes experienced the pressure of termination policy. Were the Flathead Reservation terminated, particularly the Crow and the Blackfeet Reservations with their considerable resources would have been next in line. To deal with this threat and to help solve other tribal problems, tribal councils from all seven of Montana's reservations founded the Montana Inter-Tribal Policy Board, a state-wide organization, in 1951. This was the first organization of its kind in the nation. It had two representatives from each reservation in the state and two representatives of the state's landless Indians.[79] Board members argued that the termination bills purported to solve Indian problems without considering the tremendous impact they would have upon the Indians and the state and local governments. They wanted any agreement to be bilateral, with all claims settled and a minimum of ten years of preparation time needed before withdrawal could take place.[80] In the termination bills treaty obligations had been ignored, tribal consent was missing, and the impacts on tribal, state and local welfare had not been considered.[81]

Robert Yellowtail chaired the policy board. Born in 1888, he attended Sherman Institute in Riverside, California, and graduated from Harvard with a law degree. A full-blood Crow, Yellowtail insisted that the Crows control their own affairs. In the early twentieth century he was among the tribal leaders who protected the tribe's communal lands against non-Indian encroachment. In 1915 he suggested that no tribal lands should be sold without tribal consent. He failed to get congressional backing for this proposition. At the same time Yellowtail acted as the spokesman for the Crow Business Committee. He proposed that the tribe buy cattle for every tribal member to keep more land in active tribal use. The BIA refused to help financially. Yellowtail also proposed that the tribe be given administrative control over the reservation, but the BIA agent ignored this idea. From 1934 to 1945 Yellowtail served as superintendent of the Crow Reservation. He failed to get the tribal membership to ratify the IRA due to political rivalry and the fear of an alien form of government. Many considered him too aggressive in endorsing John Collier's policies.[82]

When termination threatened Montana reservations, Yellowtail pointed out the strength of Indian unity in the state by commenting that 97 percent of Indians sent Senator Murray back to Congress and Representative D'Ewart "back to his ranch" in the 1954 elections. The Indian vote had raised the ire of D'Ewart, who charged Yellowtail was a "millionaire ward of the government," the money coming mainly from stock raising.[83] Yellowtail emphasized tribal consent to termination and suggested that a carefully constructed and decisive referendum should be conducted in each reservation over the issue.[84] He did not think that the BIA should be abolished because federal protection was needed, but the BIA should be turned over to Indians to manage and run. He further emphasized the need for individual economic rehabilitation to make Indians self-sufficient. Additional funding for education, law and order, and hospital care also were necessary.[85] Yellowtail especially objected to the 1903 U.S. Supreme Court Lone Wolf decision which allowed Congress to change Indian treaties without the consent of the tribes. According to that decision, Yellowtail complained, "The Indians have no vested rights of property in their lands; only that of occupancy with the fee in the United States . . . Congress can pass any law in conflict with Indian treaties . . . Thus, Indian treaties arn't worth the paper that they are written on."[86]

The Blackfeet Reservation seemed to be next in line if the Flathead Reservation were terminated. Recent oil finds made this action probable. David Higgins, a Blackfeet tribal and Montana House of Representatives member and the chairman of the Inter-Tribal Policy Board at the time of his testimony at termination hearings, also pointed out that treaties had been ignored. Termination would create hardship as the costs would fall entirely upon the state and counties who could not bear them and did not want to provide adequate care for Indians they considered federal wards. The bills were not well-planned nor well thought-out, Higgins concluded. A tribal referendum was needed on whether the withdrawal of federal supervision should take place or not.[87]

Rancher Higgins was one of the mixed-blood majority who historian Kenneth Philp had accused of overlooking the rights of the full-blood Blackfeet minority. The progressive mixed-blood Blackfeet business council wanted to uphold the right of self-determination under the Indian Reorganization Act, which resulted in a run-in with Commissioner Myer. Myer could not accept any piecemeal approach to self-determination and insisted that the Blackfeet work with him on a comprehensive withdrawal plan. To prove his point, Myer pointed out to the business council's alleged mishandlings of tribal money. Indeed, as was the case at Flathead, the full-blood traditionals accused the mixed-blood tribal leaders of favoritism and complained that the IRA transferred power from the traditional chiefs to the mixed-blood minority willing to "emancipate" themselves. Unlike at Flathead, the Blackfeet leaders wanted all tribal members, not just those living on the reservation, to have the right to vote in tribal referenda.[88] No doubt tribal factionalism, infighting, alleged financial unclarities, and recent oil discoveries gave Commissioner Myer and western resource interests new ammunition. Blackfeet leaders most likely were greatly relieved when termination failed at Flathead.

In contrast with the Salish and Kootenai at Flathead, whose unified leadership opposed termination and thus negated the efforts of the relatively ineffectual tribal support for the progam, the Klamaths, the Menominees, and the Utes were factionalized to an extent that limited the influence of their tribal governments. The congressional delegations of Wisconsin and Oregon did not strongly oppose the termination policy. In Utah, of course, Senator Watkins was a strong advocate of termination. Finally, too few state officials in Utah, Wisconsin, and Oregon articulated their responses to the prospect of termination.

The Klamath community offered an instructive case in contrast to the situation at Flathead. The Klamath, Modoc, and the Yahooskin Band of Snake Paiute Indians, despite being traditional enemies, had been assigned a common reservation in the Klamath Lake basin of southern Oregon. The Klamath Reservation was on the verge of economic autonomy in the 1950s, which made it vulnerable to the termination ideology. Thanks to their extensive timber resources, the Klamath tribes paid the administrative costs of the BIA by 1953. In 1957 only four Indians were on welfare. For these reasons Klamaths in later years considered termination as a nearly successful attempt to eradicate tribal culture; to acquire the 860,000 acres of Ponderosa pine, the tribes' most valuable natural resource, for the benefit of the local whites; and to abrogate and remove the bulk of federal responsibilities guaranteed to the tribes by a treaty. External pressure on tribal resources and withdrawal of the federal government's supervision further aggravated tribal divisions and caused confusion. In the 1990s, Klamath leaders argued that termination involved a major inconsistency. Despite Superintendent E. J. Diehl's and the tribes' arguments to the contrary, Congress deemed the Klamaths sophisticated enough to assimilate. At the same time the federal agencies implementing termination concluded that one half of the adult tribal members were incapable of managing their own affairs without a legal guardian. This contradiction revealed that the actual purpose of termination was to satisfy the local desire for tribal forest resources.[89] Effective tribal government proved difficult as all tribal members belonged to the governing body, the general council. A quorum was thus nearly impossible to obtain. Therefore much of the daily business fell to the eight-person business council.[90] Weak and splintered government hurt the Klamaths during the termination period.

Historian Larry Hasse argued that the Klamath Reservation, with its extensive timber resources, provided laboratory conditions for the termination policy. He asserted that both congressmen and BIA officials believed that the failure or success of the national Indian policy depended on the Klamath. Therefore they showed little sympathy toward those tribal members and leaders who opposed the policy and tried to avoid the dispersal of tribal assets.[91] Hasse's argument was a useful one; certainly congressional committees chose to ignore views that contradicted their perceptions, and negative assessments of Klamath preparedness for termination were brushed aside even after the Klamath Termination Bill passed in 1954.

Perhaps one third of the Klamath tribal members had relocated away from the reservation through the years. Most of the relocatees had begun to drift away which undermined the unity of the tribe and the reservation. This also made it difficult to determine tribal membership. Rolls were opened and closed constantly. By 1940's the tribes' 2,118 enrolled members had divided into progressive and the traditionalist factions. Wade Crawford and his wife Ida represented the majority of the progressive mixed-bloods who moved easily within the white communities and were not threatened by the possibility of termination. Born in 1895, Wade Crawford served as the superintendent of the reservation from 1933 to 1937, but fell from grace with the New Deal era and lobbied for the division of tribal assets. As early as 1929, the Crawfords had assisted Secretary of the Interior Ray Lyman Wilbur in an attempt to draw up a plan calling for the establishment of a tribal corporation to take over and manage tribal assets.[92]

Largely due to Wade Crawford's efforts, Senator Hugh Butler introduced the Klamath termination bill in 1947. Senator Wayne Morse of Oregon did not have a final position on the merits of the bill, but believed that through an educational process Indians would be ready. That bill was not passed, but the Klamath Termination Bill, PL 587 as a law, found success in 1954. In the congressional hearings on that bill, Wade Crawford assured the committee members that the disposal of tribal assets would be a positive development. Crawford had lost an election to the tribal council and could not testify as a tribal delegate. In an unusual move, the BIA paid for his trip to the hearings.[93] Ida Crawford accused the tribal leadership of being "a mouthpiece of the Indian Bureau." Much like Lorena Burgess at Flathead, the Crawfords thought that the reservation government was communistic and un-American. They wanted to liquidate tribal assets through a sale for cash to the highest bidder as soon as possible. This, they argued, would be "the only fair, logical, American way to settle the Klamath estate."[94]

Boyd Jackson, one of the leaders of the tribal business committee, led the traditionalists and cooperated with federal officials to limit the Crawfords' influence. In 1947 Jackson articulated his hopes that Congress would come up with a more positive plan, which would include optional withdrawal and payment of shares to those who so wished. He knew that tribal members could not both withdraw and retain an interest in the tribe.[95] Jackson did not realize that his careful words could be taken as an approval of termination. Still, he opposed early liquidation as economically and socially unadvisable and preferred that the reservation remain intact as a unit which Indians would operate without BIA control. Brothers Seldon and Jesse Lee Kirk led the tribes' general council and business committee respectively. Both belonged to the traditionalist faction. They largely concurred with Jackson. Seldon Kirk, a carpenter, favored termination if a majority of tribal members approved the plan. The tribes did not have this option, so Kirk turned against termination in any form.[96]

The Kirks argued that the 1947 bill was designed for the sole purpose of securing more taxes for the state. They labeled the bill "a blatantly foul scheme to cheat and rob." These tribal leaders assured the reservation superintendent that the Klamath tribes were not demanding their independence.[97] Forrest Cooper, the counsel for the Interstate Association of Public Land Counties, had prepared the rough draft of the Klamath termination bill that the Kirks so condemned. Cooper admitted that the bill was written to please the county governments. He recommended that the lands in tribal ownership, "the surplus lands," should be offered for sale for cash at a public auction instead of being purchased by the federal government.[98] This provision fortunately did not appear in either the Butler bill of 1947 or PL 587 of 1954.

Not realizing that it would provide an additional incentive for termination, the Klamath general council in May 1951 gave its consent for Oregon to assume jurisdiction on the reservation to help resolve juvenile delinquency problems and to save the tribes money. In 1954 the Klamath general council conditionally accepted the proposed termination bill as withdrawal seemed inevitable, but they tried to change the bill to allow for more self-determination.[99] In the hearings, the elected tribal delegates expressed their opposition to termination, wanting more time and study to find out whether the plan had a chance to work. However, Wade Crawford urged liquidation without delay and claimed that 95-98 percent of tribal members were capable of taking care of themselves.[100] Klamath opinion was badly divided, and a skillful manipulator such as Senator Watkins was able to make it appear that they did not entirely oppose the termination of their reservation. Watkins cooperated with the Crawfords and treated the elected tribal representatives, who opposed his views, with contempt. To pressure the Klamath tribes, Senator Watkins seized the opportunity to withhold congressional approval for a $2.6 million claims award payment until the elected leaders agreed to termination.[101]

With termination, the Klamath tribes were divided into "withdrawing members" and "remaining members." As there was little useful information about the real meaning of either choice, nor any information about the management of the remaining assets, many thought they could get both money and land. PL 587 required that three management specialists guard the tribal assets left after the withdrawing members got their shares. In a 1955 referendum Seldon Kirk, Wade Crawford, and Laurence Witte were elected to a committee dealing with the specialists. The other members were all local bankers and businessmen. This election assured tribal cooperation with specialists, as progressives had a two to one majority on the committee.[102] The management specialists soon realized that the Klamaths were not ready for termination and that a federal purchase of the tribally owned assets would be the best way to assure the long-term interests of the remaining members. Only at this point did the state of Oregon wake up to protest termination at Klamath.[103] Indeed, the United States Forest Service bought most of the tribal forest lands for 90 million dollars and made them a part of Winema National Forest. The additional cost for welfare expenditures and other new federal investments undermined the argument of those who supported termination as a means of saving the government money.

The Crawford faction opposed the amendment to postpone termination from 1958, as PL 587 stated, to 1961. Senator Richard Neuberger of Oregon favored the delay, not because of tribal unpreparedness for withdrawal of federal services, but because he feared the effects on the local economy of dumping so much timber on the market. He also concluded that the termination plan was too hasty in only giving the Klamath tribes one alternative, that of selling their assets. Neuberger admitted that lumber companies, who had been seeking access to tribal forests, would be, and indeed turned out to be, the only beneficiaries of Klamath termination.[104]

It appeared that the younger tribal members generally supported liquidation for its promised financial benefits. They believed that they were getting nothing for their money under the old system. The older members were more ambivalent.

Many did not fully understand what termination would actually mean. As at Flathead, many Klamaths believed that the BIA wasted tribal money, and that the tribes were fully capable of taking care of themselves. A majority of the tribal members wanted to withdraw but also thought that it would be a good idea to keep the reservation lands intact after termination, yet no planning was made to that effect. As management plans were vague and slow, members had no confidence in that option and chose to withdraw instead.[105] On the other hand, many opposed the withdrawal plan, and the business council argued government assistance was needed before termination would be possible. They felt that the termination bills were illogical and unconstitutional, and were neither introduced nor sponsored by the tribe. In addition, Jackson and his associates feared that the treaties would be dissolved without tribal consent and that the majority of tribal members were not ready to assume full personal responsibility. The reality of local racial prejudice also caused alarm.[106]

The Klamaths suffered two kinds of losses. The tangible assets lost were the forests and tribal lands. Klamath economic self-sufficiency had depended on revenues generated primarily by tribal timber and industries. The withdrawing members got an immediate return in the form of a cash payment. Seventy-eight percent or 1,659 tribal members chose to withdraw and take the cash. Under this arrangement each person received $43,000. However, only 34 percent of the withdrawing members received their share without restrictions. Most people spent this sum quickly and so liquidation led to the end of self-sufficiency and the start of dependency. It turned out to be impossible for the tribes and individual tribal members to purchase any of the lands: Acquisition could only be in blocks of at least five thousand acres.[107]

The intangible loss was the Klamath identity as an Indian nation. This loss caused incalculable psychological damage. Those born after August 13, 1954, were no longer members of the Klamath tribes. Tribal members did not have checking accounts and most depended on per capita payments for their income. Once these were gone, dependency on welfare soon followed. The whole culture was forced to undergo significant change, the economy was destroyed, the social fabric was spent, and tribal government authority was undermined. No wonder that many felt guilt and frustration and turned to alcoholism and violence. After termination, the average Klamath died too young, at the median age of only 43. Seventy per cent did not graduate from high school. Most were poor.[108] Eventually the Klamath Restoration Act of 1986 provided for a return of federal services, but it did not truly restore the reservation because the land base was gone.

The situation at Menominee also was instructive. Like the Flathead and Klamath Reservations, the Menominee Reservation of Wisconsin contained significant timber resources. Menominee thus found itself on part one of Acting Commissioner William Zimmerman's 1947 list as a reservation ready for immediate termination. Nicholas Peroff argued that the tribe was a pawn in a congressional experiment. There was a widespread belief, probably due to the influence of a few members of the tribal elite, that the tribe wanted termination, and that this course of action was for the benefit of tribal members. Only on the eve of the final deadline did the Senate subcommittee acknowledge that not all tribal members were completely prepared, but it was unwilling to turn back.[109] The Menominee held various opinions about why their reservation was terminated. Some believed that it was because they were doing well, others thought that the old management system was too communistic, many concluded that the elite had sold them out, and still others thought that signs of progressiveness and independence influenced the termination decision. There were those who believed that religious differences caused termination. The tribe, largely Catholic, had thrown the Mormons off the reservation, which, some thought, earned

Senator Watkins' wrath. In any event, Watkins said that the tribe would be terminated whether it wanted it or not.[110]

Clearly, then, the Menominee tribe lacked unity. A political elite of some five per cent of tribal members, members of a few families, controlled the reservation politically and economically. They were disproportionately wealthy and well-educated. This group believed that termination would be beneficial in the long run and reluctantly accepted the BIA's termination plan to get per capita payments, which obviously could help their personal businesses. The elite shared a consensus based upon middle-class white American values rather than on the traditional culture of the Menominee Indian.[111]

Ninety percent of the Menominees originally were inactive and even apathetic on the issue of termination, but later many of them joined the small group which opposed this change. However, widespread opposition did not emerge until termination was well on the way. The prospect of federal withdrawal increased internal conflict between the elite and the others.[112] Divisions between the elite and other tribal members and between the on-reservation and off-reservation residents weakened tribal leadership. Just as had happened at Klamath, the Menominees experienced a leadership crisis, which played into the hands of the terminationists.[113]

After initially subsiding in 1947, the threat of termination returned in 1951, when Congress appropriated $8.5 million as a compromise settlement to a suit filed by the tribe in 1935 alleging BIA mismanagement of tribal assets. Commissioner Myer then began urging the tribe to prepare for termination and refused to authorize the per capita distribution of $1,500 from this award unless a comprehensive withdrawal plan was prepared. At this point, the governing elite adopted a strategy of reluctant approval of termination while pushing for a per capita distribution. Eventually it gave up opposing the withdrawal completely, believing it inevitable.[114]

The state of Wisconsin did not really oppose federal withdrawal at Menominee. Governor Walter J. Kohler, Jr., seemed to support the move toward assimilation and only cautioned that more time was needed for the transition. Tax Commissioner Harry Harder represented the state in the 1954 hearings. Harder admitted that state officials thought that termination had already been decided and doubted the importance of their opinions. This conclusion clearly was a mistake, as the example of Montana demonstrated. Instead of trying to kill the Menominee termination bill, Wisconsin only tried to win more time for preparation. Although the state was wary of the effects, it also wanted to protect its treasury. Therefore it recommended the preservation of tribal forest resources.[115]

Wisconsin congressmen failed to voice their opposition to termination even when they felt some of its effects might be harmful. Representative Henry Reuss wanted special arrangements to protect the tribe from state taxation; otherwise he thought it would be fatal for the tribal forests.[116] Representative John Byrnes wanted a more thorough study, after which he declared he would be in favor of termination.[117] Only Representative Melvin Laird opposed the policy. This may have been because the Menominee Reservation was in his district. He considered the proposed bill as unacceptable because it broke the treaty and lacked tribal consent. Laird also argued that the state had been contacted late, and he objected to the tribe having to agree to pay half of the expenses to terminate its own reservation in order to win an extension from 1958 to 1960. Senator Alexander Wiley concurred with that opinion and asked for a further extension because of emerging difficulties.[118]

The Menominee tribe and Congressman Laird believed that termination was inevitable. As Laird had urged, the tribe passed a resolution in July 1953 accepting a termination bill of its own as a substitute to the bill Senator Watkins preferred. Growing fear about the consequences of termination eventually inspired more opposition to it, but these doubts surfaced too late. After a couple of postponements, Menominee termination took effect on June 30, 1961.[119] The Menominee Reservation turned into Menominee County, the smallest in population and poorest of all counties in Wisconsin. It could not cover all of its administrative expenses. It had to close the BIA hospital, which did not meet state standards. The state was reluctant to grant special aid to the county and the federal government had to support the county to prevent its bankruptcy. Once again, termination at Menominee did not save federal dollars. Indeed quite the opposite took place. The Menominees refused to accept termination. After a successful drive by tribal rights group, Determination for Rights and Unity for Menominee Shareholders (DRUMS), the reservation was restored in 1973.[120] Based on the Menominee Fairness Act of 1999, Congress in August of 1999 awarded the Menominee tribe 27 million dollars as compensation for the actions of the federal government and Congress during termination.

If the Flathead, the Menominee, and the Klamath were on the list of terminated reservations because of their ample resources, the six bands of Utah Paiutes and the Uintah-Ouray Reservation of Utah were on the list of terminated reservations for entirely different reasons. They had the misfortune of being situated in the home state of Senator Watkins who wanted to avoid accusations of parochial politics. The Uintah-Ouray termination followed a similar pattern of serving as a pre-condition to releasing a claims award of $32 million. The Paiute bands were small and scattered and lacked the funds to hire attorneys to defend themselves.[121] Still, Watkins did not manage to terminate Utah reservations at will, even if the state officials agreed with him and his fellow congressmen did not bother to oppose him. Various tribal groups in the state of Utah, the targets of his policy, did raise objections. Of the six Southern Paiute bands, two consistently opposed termination and were dropped from the bill, thus avoiding the fate the Klamaths and the Menominees suffered.[122]

Watkins came to Congress after a career as a lawyer in Vernal, a small community located near the Uintah-Ouray Reservation in eastern and northeastern Utah. This reservation was a home for 1,765 Uintahs, Uncompahgre Utes, and Whiteriver Utes. Like at Flathead and Klamath, then, the reservation consisted of three unrelated bands which disliked each other. The largely mixed-blood Uintahs were the original occupants of the reservation, to which the other groups had been relocated later from Colorado. The old animosity was still present in the 1950s and contributed to some tribal members' attitudes towards termination. Termination pressure increased factionalism, distrust, and the fight over the award money between the bands. The long-term plan to use the award seemed to favor the mixed-bloods.[123]

Termination at Uintah-Ouray essentially represented an experiment by legislation, which assumed that quantum of blood was a measure of Indian competence. Senator Watkins considered all Indians of one half or less Indian blood as non-Indians. Facing resistance to his termination plans at Uintah-Ouray he came up with a plan to terminate mixed blood tribal members. These were mostly Uintahs, who had a long history of incorporating members of other tribes into their social structure and now were punished for it. Only 57 percent of the Uintahs were one-half blood or more. Tribal attorney John Boyden, a Mormon like Watkins, pressured mixed blood tribal members, largely Utes, to cooperate with the senator in order to keep their reservation and lands intact. The tribal council voted to restrict tribal membership to those who could prove that they had at minimum one-half Indian blood. The Ute delegates to congressional hearings were carefully chosen to include supporters of termination. Watkins later added a clause to the bill which stated that to avoid termination, and to remain an enrolled member, one had to have more than 50 percent Indian blood. This provision made termination in the future inevitable for all tribal members.[124] This policy remained in place until Congress ended the entire termination policy in 1968.

The effects for the 490 terminated mixed-bloods turned out to be just as disastrous as elsewhere. They had to sell their share of tribal assets to the tribes and no longer had access to tribal land to graze their cattle, which made earning a livelihood difficult. The termination act implied that they needed help, so private banks managed their assets. They lost their status as Indians and were no longer entitled to federal services for tribal members. Cultural differences made it impossible to adapt to non-Indian world in the given time of seven years. The result was unemployment, poverty, alcoholism, and the loss of identity.[125]

In conclusion, whether a specific reservation avoided termination depended on three factors. Even if factionalized, the tribe or tribes occupying a reservation could mount a concerted effort to oppose it with the help of an effective attorney. Tribal members could point to the treaties and could manage to demonstrate the negative effects of termination. For this argument to be persuasive, the state had to be sympathetic to the tribes. Finally congressional representatives had to join in the opposition. As termination legislation went through a consent calendar, even a little opposition could defeat the bills. In the case of the Flathead Reservation, the hard work of the tribal council of the Salish and Kootenai tribes combined with significant state and congressional opposition to termination halted the process. As we have seen, the Klamaths of Oregon, the Menominees of Wisconsin, and the Uintah-Ouray Uintahs of Utah could not claim the same degree of unity and termination eventually took place on these reservations.

Chapter 4

After Termination: Salish and Kootenai Self-Determination

We have seen how the Salish and Kootenai tribes of the Flathead Reservation successfully resisted termination in the 1950s. However, the idea of withdrawal of federal supervision from the reservation did not disappear from tribal life at that time and neither did tribal factionalism. Still, the decades from the mid-1950s to the present have been a time of increasing self-determination and independence for the Salish and Kootenai peoples. This chapter deals with the issues of enrollment, Indian-white conflict, factionalism and liquidation of tribal assets after 1954. The debate and struggle over these and other issues have made the tribes a nation governed by a modern representative government which has control over its economy and allows no non-Indian infringements on its sovereignty. The development leading to this situation has not been easy nor simple, but it showed that determined and capable tribal government can achieve a number of things even if it had to battle heavy opposition from its neighbors and from within its own ranks.

Termination policy in part contributed to the rise of American Indian ethnic renewal in the 1960s. That result was unintended. Sociologist Joane Nagel argued that assimilationist policies in the form of termination and relocation inadvertently promoted demographic and organizational changes that led to the rise of activism, ethnic identification, and cultural renaissance. Increased education led to student interaction,

World War II created a new sense of pan-Indianism, Indian New Deal programs spurred intertribal contact, and the Indian Claims Commission process revitalized the sense of tribal community. All these influences encouraged American Indians to work for a change in policy away from termination and towards self-determination. Nagel concluded that the congressional change of heart was due to the failure of termination and better organized tribal opposition to that policy.[1]

George Castile and James Rawls argued that Indian tribes utilized the new opportunities created by President Lyndon B. Johnson's Office of Economic Opportunity programs. Those much-criticized tribal governments created by the Indian Reorganization Act were ready when the War on Poverty funds were made available. Community Action Programs allowed tribes to design their own plans and bypass the Bureau of Indian Affairs and shift power from the superintendents to the tribal governments. On the other hand, Castile argued, these programs made many tribes even more dependent on the federal government. Finally President Richard M. Nixon's New Federalism renounced HCR 108 and the termination policy.[2] Certainly these arguments hold true for the Salish and Kootenai of the Flathead Reservation. As one current tribal elder noted, the tribes' assertiveness started in the 1960s, in part due to the expansion of the civil rights struggle.[3]

There are seven Indian reservations in Montana. Their combined land area totals 8.3 million acres or nine per cent of the total land mass in the state. The Flathead Reservation today has 1,316,871 acres, of which 740,000 or 56 percent is in tribal ownership and a mere 3.1 percent is owned by individual Indians. The tribes have consistently repurchased individual allotments. The Confederated Salish and Kootenai Tribes had 6,832 enrolled members in 1995. The total Indian population on the reservation was 5,130, but only some 3,500 of them were enrolled members of the Salish and Kootenai tribes. Twenty-four percent of the reservation population of 21,259 (1998) were Indians. Forty-one percent of tribal members living on the reservation were listed as unemployed in 1995, 26.7 percent of adults over 25 years of age had no high school diploma, and the median yearly household income among on-reservation Indian families was just under $20,000, nearly $10,000 below that of local whites. In all 22.8 percent of tribal members were counted as being below the federal poverty level. These figures showed that resources had not brought wealth to tribal members. It is important to note that the Salish and Kootenai had the lowest unemployment and poverty rates, the best educational level, and the second highest median income of any Montana reservation.[4]

Of the nearly 7,000 tribal members, only 1.5 percent were full-bloods by the late 1980s and twenty-five per cent were at or below ¼ blood, the current requirement for tribal enrollment. Psychologist Theresa O'Nell has addressed the fact that it has become increasingly problematic to define what it meant to be an Indian. Enrollment had been a very divisive issue from the 1930s to the present. Enrollment had particularly caused tensions between the full- and mixed-bloods. On the other hand, inter-marriages were common and the matter of Indian descent had become more complicated, with many tribal descendants now ineligible for tribal membership. Some family members could be enrolled while others were not. Blood-quantum remained important, even though, as O'Nell argued, being enrolled and being recognized as an Indian were two different things. One could participate in the community even if one was not enrolled. However, tribal services were free only for the enrolled.[5]

Federal withdrawal had remained a threat after the termination bills of 1954 were defeated. Congressman James Haley of Florida, chairman of the House Indian Affairs Subcommittee, in 1957 reminded Secretary Fred Seaton that HCR 108 was still in effect. Prompted by this reminder, the BIA Billings Area Director argued that the bureau desired that tribes themselves initiate the planning for termination, but this time without any specific time limit. He thought that it would be better to accept the policy and to work it out on an orderly basis rather than to devote energy toward resisting it. Area Director Percy Melis pointed out that should the Salish and Kootenai tribes fail to develop their own program, Congress might take action on its own. He argued that the first step was to accept the inevitability of termination; once this step was taken, things could be worked out. Tribal leaders were not persuaded. Vice-Chairman Walter Morigeau contended that accepting termination would automatically liquidate the treaty of 1855 and that lifting trust restrictions would lead to high corporate taxes and loss of assets. He pointed out that when the tribes attempted to do their own planning on anything, the BIA interfered.[6] With the congressional mood changing by the early 1960s, local BIA officials stopped talking about termination, even if they wanted the tribes to run their own affairs. Harold Roberson, reservation superintendent in the late 1960s, wanted the tribes to take over BIA's duties, but insisted that the trust relationship be maintained.[7]

In the meeting with Area Director Melis, Vice-Chairman Walter Morigeau said that he had earlier proposed a plan whereby the federal government would buy all tribal assets at their appraised value, and the tribes would close their rolls and then grant equal shares to all enrolled members. Over a period of twenty years the government would purchase the remaining interest held in trust. In this manner the liquidation of tribal assets could be made gradual and with very little hardship to the members. Chairman Walter McDonald emphasized that since the federal government was instrumental in termination, it should take some responsibility for the expenses. He also wanted to know why there was no program to rehabilitate the tribes before termination, so they could be ready.[8]

Steve DeMers, a Salish Kootenai tribal member residing in Butte, Montana, and an active participant in discussions about the Indian future, addressed the issue of termination in an address he gave in 1960. He repeated the same arguments that he and other tribal council members had made in the 1954 hearings. Before termination could take effect, several minimum requirements should be fulfilled: Any agreement should be bilateral with no threat of coercion, all claims should be settled, the federal government should assist in negotiations with the state and county governments, a complete survey and inventory of resources was needed, a minimum of ten years of planning would be required, and both parties should have access to the U.S. Court of Appeals. DeMers thought that anything less than these minimum conditions would result in chaos. He understood the need to develop forward-looking programs that would improve the social and economic abilities of all Indians, so that they could be ready to assume more responsibility for services.[9]

Through the Governors' Interstate Indian Council, the governors in western states had generally supported assimilation, if not termination. They became more cautious once the problems with the Klamath and Menominee terminations began to appear. In 1961, John Reynolds, the Attorney General of Wisconsin, emphasized the need to have tribal input in any planning affecting the future of the tribes. Indians should be well prepared before any termination planning could be done, he concluded.[10] The directors of the Indian Affairs departments of the participating states contended that complete studies needed to be made of tribal preparedness and state readiness for the new status. State-tribal cooperation and acceptance should be achieved, the role of taxation must be understood, and per capita payments needed to be de-emphasized before any termination plans could be concluded. The governors stressed that the termination of trusteeship was different from the termination of services; the latter should not take place. No haste nor force should be used, and any termination plan should provide for orderly withdrawal.[11] In a 1960 resolution, the governors declared that HCR 108 should be interpreted as an objective, not an immediate goal. Before termination, Indians' educational level should be equal to that of whites. Federal aid was needed to achieve this goal.[12]

Economic opportunity for non-Indians helped encourage the drive to terminate the Flathead Reservation in the 1950s. White people for generations had sought ways to gain access to the reservation. One current tribal elder thought that newcomers did not want Indians around and "want to terminate us."[13] The termination idea has on occasion come up from outside the tribe, mostly from state and congressional politicians, but has died out. In the 1990s the State of Montana and the tribes were in conflict over Highway 93, which passes through the reservation. This heavily traveled road had two lanes, but local interests wanted it expanded to four lanes. The tribes opposed this change. Tribal elders saw this conflict as an example of why local politicians would like to get the tribes terminated: It would remove an impediment to local development.[14] Montana's former United States Senator Conrad Burns, a Republican, had supported non-Indian majority rule and considered reservations states within states, of which he disapproved. He introduced a bill to give non-Indian farmers unconditional control over tribally run irrigation and power systems in the Flathead Reservation.[15] Thurman Trosper argued that Burns' proposal to give up some tribal authority to the state could be the first step towards the eventual termination of the reservation. Burns had to withdraw his irrigation bill when Indians stormed the hearings held in Montana in protest.[16]

The relationship between the tribal members and the reservation non-Indians had at times been tense and filled with conflict. The antagonism had increased when the tribes attempted to increase their control of the reservation or had passed a resolution which regulated non-Indian activities. Non-Indians often complained, and still do, about lack of participation in a government that regulates them.[17] Trouble had been brewing between non-Indians and the tribes throughout their common history, but relations became particularly tense in the 1970s, the decade when the tribes really began to assert their self-determination and the right to regulate non-Indian activities on tribal property. Many locals expressed their worry about the deterioration of relations between the parties: "The old-timers are about all gone, the newcomers are not informed & tempers are beginning to flare," one observed.[18] One local resident had a long list of grievances against the tribes and the BIA, blaming them for the increasing tensions. He argued that those "non-Indian" tribal members who were less than half-blood got all the benefits, while the half- to full-bloods, some of whom really needed help, should have been the intended beneficiaries.[19] Another local non-Indian was jealous of tribal members of low Indian blood: "They receive free schooling, medical & dental expenses, free commodities, free hot lunches, and they cry discrimination!" This person also complained that any deeded land that Indians bought back could be put into trust and become tax-free causing a heavier tax-burden on non-Indians.[20] Others urged that all Indian reservations be dissolved in fairness to both Indians and non-Indians because "reservations have out-lived their usefulness and their continued existence is bringing about inequalities to all." To these non-Indians, the Flathead Reservation was a seedbed of "'red power' activism," where most tribal members of limited Indian blood received services tax free.[21] These comments showed the unfortunate ignorance that many local residents had of tribal rights and limitations of living on an Indian reservation.

John Crow, the Deputy Commissioner of Indian Affairs, had to reply to these fears. He thought that the problems had developed because the tribal council had enacted legislation — Ordinance 44-A Revised in 1969 — to establish a permit system pertaining to the management of land and other tribal resources, which, despite being proper and within the council's authority, had caused much controversy. The tribes threatened to close all recreational areas to non-Indian use because the enforcement of tribal regulations was difficult, litigation slow, and, above all, non-tribal members failed to observe tribal regulations. While the tribes did not follow through on their threat to close non-Indian access to reservation's recreational sites, they collected fees, which created a lot of objections. Crow noted that according to the Indian Reorganization Act of 1934, the BIA gave preference to Indians in employment. To the accusations of low blood quanta among tribal members, Crow replied that the tribes had a full right to determine their own membership.[22]

As Deputy Commissioner Crow noted, water rights issues pitted tribal interests in natural resources against the irrigation interests of local non-Indian farmers and ranchers. The tribes had retained treaty rights to the land lying below the high water mark on the southern half of Flathead Lake and imposed regulations on the use of this area from 1970. The City Council of Polson and Polson Chamber of Commerce passed motions objecting to any action that would close the south half of the Flathead Lake and other previously unrestricted waters, citing severe adverse economic impacts on the growing tourism business and irreparable harm and polarization between Indians and non-Indians.[23] The city got support from one longtime non-tribal lake shore resident, who considered the permit-system a tribute, which was extremely unfair, unjustified and would seriously affect the steadily increasing tourist and recreational business.[24] Former BIA official and tribal secretary Thomas "Bearhead" Swaney claimed that the controversy over the use permit only "brought out what has always been there."[25]

The tribes followed their regulation of the southern half of the Flathead Lake with the tribal Shoreline Protection Ordinance of 1977. The City of Polson challenged the tribal right to enact lake shore regulation in court, arguing that tribal water rights had been extinguished by the allotment act of 1904. The State of Montana concurred. While the federal district court agreed with the challenge, the Ninth Circuit Court overturned the case in favor of the tribes in 1982. The court ruled that the state did not have jurisdiction over Indian water rights and recognized tribal regulatory powers over non-Indians. The negative consequence of the tribal victory was continued ill-feeling between the tribes and local non-Indians. To ease tensions, the tribes provided for three non-Indians to act as voting members on the seven-person Shoreline Protection Board, whose chair was nonvoting.[26] The Salish and Kootenai established a Natural Resources Department in 1981 and passed a tribal water code that same year. According to the code, each user was required to file a plan of water use. However, the federal government hesitated to approve the plan because it would threaten the welfare of non-Indians. After continuous litigation, the federal district court in 1996 ruled that the tribes had the right to regulate water use on the reservation.[27]

The struggle over reservation jurisdiction, resources, and the limits of tribal sovereignty led to the founding of overtly racist groups such as Montanans Opposing Discrimination (MOD), which evolved into All Citizens Equal (ACE). Two outspoken leaders of the anti-sovereignty forces were Delbert Palmer and William H. Covey, both white residents of the Flathead Reservation. Palmer was arrested for hunting on his land without a permit from the tribes, but he refused to recognize the authority of the tribal government. Soon after moving onto the reservation, Covey found out that he could be prosecuted in tribal court if he violated either tribal or federal laws. Both joined MOD. This group stated that its purpose was to "prevent unjust and unreasonable discrimination against any citizen . . . regardless of race, creed or national origin." MOD sought to end practices that it believed favored Indians. It claimed a membership of 3,000 on or near the reservation. The backlash leaders insisted that they were forced to obey tribal ordinances that they had no voice in creating. ACE argued that Indians of small blood quantities were enjoying unreasonable privileges.[28] Covey's case was typical: He moved into the reservation without understanding that he could be subject to tribal jurisdiction, and instead of submitting to reservation rules he reacted by crying foul.

As the president of ACE, Covey met backlash leaders from other states and formed the Citizens Equal Rights Alliance (CERA) in March 1988. An umbrella organization for the national anti-sovereignty movement, CERA claimed more than 500,000 supporters from 22 states, including real estate interests, agribusinesses, and mining companies, who felt threatened by the tribes' growing control over their resources. Covey condemned the idea that "Indian country" included fee simple lands on reservations and that tribal governments possessed jurisdiction over individuals living on such holdings. Aiming to overhaul the legal system for Indian affairs, CERA sent representatives to lobby Congress. According to historian Donald Parman, Covey's ideas reflected a typical western perspective: A dislike of government control but a desire for government help when problems appear.[29] Native American leaders believed that racism and jealousy were the root causes of the white backlash against tribal governments: "They were comfortable thinking of the poor halfwit Indian. Now that we are taking control of our assets they are just in shock."[30]

It must be noted that the perspective of those non-Indians whose families had lived on the reservation for decades had been considerably more moderate than that of Covey and ACE. There were those who supported tribal sovereignty. "Neighbors" was a group of Flathead Reservation-area residents, who "promote communication and cooperation between and among tribal and non-tribal people and institutions on the reservation." "Neighbors" took a firm stand in support of tribal sovereignty. The group acknowledged that the reservation was a sovereign territory that the Salish Kootenai nation retained when it ceded over twelve million acres in the 1855 Hell Gate Treaty. "Neighbors" supported the right of Indian tribes to decide the definition of sovereignty they choose for legal and ethical reasons. The organization understood that tribes with the strongest cultural integrity were most often those with the fullest political and economic control over their land base. Sovereignty meant tribal power to enact and enforce laws within reservation boundaries as well as the power to define tribal membership. "Neighbors" argued that the minority challenging treaty obligations and tribal sovereignty "continued in the tradition of ignorance, ethnocentrism, racism and/or greed" and blocked the possibility of communication and cooperation between the Salish Kootenai tribes and non-Indians on the reservation. "Neighbors" wanted to remind people that living on the reservation was politically different, which should be acknowledged before moving in.[31]

"Optional Withdrawal" Proposals of 1971 and 1984

Persistent problems with income distribution, poverty, and expected Indian Claims Commission and Court of Claims award payments led to calls to terminate the reservation and to liquidate the tribal assets in 1971, this time from *within* the tribes. Again, financial benefits prompted talk of termination, which this time did not mean abolishment of tribal status for all, but only those voluntarily leaving the tribes. However, in reality, the cost of paying off those wanting to cash in their share of tribal assets would lead to serious repercussions for the tribes, including the possibility of re-opening the door to federal termination of services, which most tribal members perceived as a real threat. On- and off-reservation tribal members were among those wanting to liquidate tribal assets, especially the timber resources. E. W. "Bill" Morigeau, a tribal council member since 1961 and its chairman from 1961 to 1963, was the leading liquidation proponent. A $6 million out of court settlement in the tribes' general accounting claim against the federal government initially prompted Morigeau's action. In Resolution 3083 the tribes in December 1970 approved the settlement. The big question was how to spend the money. The tribes' Washington, D.C., attorney, Richard Baenen, suggested that several avenues of action were open, but "The law states that no money to satisfy a judgment against the U.S. by an Indian tribe can be spent without legislation by congress. If legislation is to go through promptly a presentation must be planned in advance, also approval from the BIA must be obtained for the judgment distribution planning. Such a plan could include anything from total per capita distribution to no pay out at all."[32]

The tribal council, chaired by Salish Fred Whitworth since 1969, proposed investing at least some of the money for the future. Morigeau insisted that all of the claim money should be distributed to the membership. Therefore he insisted that all adults be "paid in full," and underage minors get their funds "placed in a special interest-bearing account" in the U.S. Treasury.[33] A successful businessman, Morigeau did not speak Salish, was comfortable in the non-Indian world, and saw the tribal council's role exclusively as a moneymaking operation. Interestingly, his rhetoric about the ineffectiveness of the council and the need to distribute all tribal income to the membership appealed to the general membership, especially those desperately poor or marginally Indian. After all, tribal leadership traditionally held its position because of its ability to distribute goods to the tribal membership. This dynamic between "progressive businessmen" and "traditionals" would label the next three decades of debate over the multiple meanings of liquidation and termination in tribal politics. Both sides would use the terms *termination* or *liquidation*, in opposite ways, in order to rally their supporters against the opposing faction.

Morigeau used an estimate of $193 million for the value of tribal assets.[34] Morigeau established a Termination of Poverty Committee, which utilized these figures and the award payments to advocate liquidation of tribal holdings and an equal cash payment to each tribal member. Despite their initial optimism, Morigeau and his supporters would fail to gain signatures from thirty percent of the tribal members eligible to vote in order to

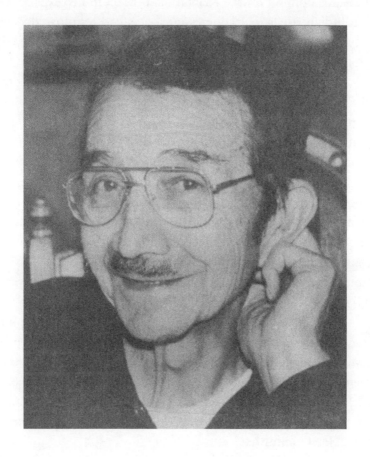

E. W. "Bill" Morigeau

Source: Confedrated Salish and Kootenai Tribes,
Pablo, Montana.

get the issue to a referendum. Baenen concluded that liquidation would make "the rich get richer and the poor get poorer." He based his opinion on the Klamath and Menominee experiences, two Indian tribes that congressional acts had terminated.[35] The tribal council took a nine-to-one stand against liquidation, with Morigeau providing the dissenting vote.

On January 10, 1971, Morigeau and Ray Courville organized a meeting in the reservation community of Polson to discuss a proposal to "liquidate resources." A somewhat misleading report in the *Missoulian* indicated that "the effort is intended as a move to terminate the Flathead Reservation as such." The newspaper further reported that "A tentative petition drawn up by Morigeau calls for the formation of a committee representing the tribal membership to draft legislation for liquidation which would be presented to Congress." The Termination of Poverty Committee consisted of 18 members, chaired temporarily by Steve DeMers. Committee members emphasized that "termination of poverty" did not mean "termination of the reservation."[36]

Immediately Salish Joe McDonald protested the liquidation as a "tremendous blow." "It would be tragic sight to see our own Indian people five years after the $35,000 [sic] was given to them. Their identity gone, their land . . . unavailable to them." McDonald thought that Termination of Indian Poverty Committee might be more aptly titled Operation Hopelessness, Despair, Genocide Committee.[37]

On January 21, the tribal council voted 9 to 1 to distribute 90 percent of the six million dollar December 1970 award money in per capita payments, which came to about $4,000 per member. In the meeting, Morigeau's motives for calling for liquidation "were questioned by other members of the council who concluded investigation of the motives should be made." Morigeau wanted to distribute 100 percent of the award, but the council moved to impeach him for "acting against tribal constitution" with his committee.[38]

Morigeau and DeMers agreed that the Termination of Poverty "movement [was] being supported by tribal members who [were] not satisfied with the way council [had] managed tribal government." They claimed that the tribes had "agreed through a resolution that the tribal council would provide a 'buy-out program' for older members who wanted to take their share" of the award money, but the council "did not act on this." Liquidation was to be accomplished through a referendum and congressional legislation. Morigeau and DeMers assured that they "would ask for hunting and fishing rights to be continued." They noted that "the method of liquidation could be patterned after the Klamath tribe," which seemed quite alarming considering the problems linked to Klamath termination, such as short-term purchases without long-term benefits, problems which DeMers must have been aware of.[39] The liquidation committee on January 20 approved a petition calling for a referendum on the issue, estimating "total tribal resources at $193 million," referring to the BIA calculations.[40]

After meeting stiff opposition, Morigeau then modified his proposal to an optional withdrawal plan, which would allow retention of mineral rights on tribal lands and hunting and fishing privileges for those opting to take their share of tribal assets in cash. On January 26, 1971, the Committee for Optional Withdrawal sent a petition letter to nearly one thousand tribal members asking for a referendum vote on liquidation. According to Morigeau, his committee had several organizing meetings in which people expressed their opinions regarding optional withdrawal. The new, rewritten petition was drafted "the way people wanted it." The petition requested "that the secretary of the interior or his authorized representatives call for a vote on the question of distributing tribal assets on a pro-rata basis, and asks for an election to amend the tribal constitution to conform to the voting laws of the State of Montana, which would allow 19 year olds to vote." The petition further asked for distribution of "the pro-rata share of the appraised value of tribal assets, including monetary settlements and judgment funds accruing, for any enrolled member desiring to withdraw their share of the tribal corporation in cash." Finally, "members would retain their interest in any mineral rights reserved on tribal lands and also retain their tribal identity to the extent of hunting and fishing privileges." Ray Dupuis of Polson resigned from the committee at this point because he could not see "buying out the Indians who want to sell and still let them have the same rights as those of us who want to remain as a member of a unified tribe."[41] This proposal clearly would have meant termination of the tribes, as it was hard to see how the tribes could have survived after buying out a large number of tribal members, nor was it realistic to expect that Congress would have accepted tribal members' retaining certain privileges after selling out.

The tribal council organized another community meeting in Dixon on January 30 to discuss liquidation. The meeting was contentious. More than four hundred tribal members, two hundred off-reservation and two hundred on-reservation Indians, attended the meeting held in a gym; most opposed the proposal. According to newspaper reports, many argued that the members would be "selling out their heritage," while others noted that "without a land base, the Indians would lose their identity." There was persistent "speculation that 'big money and big business' [were] behind the movement." Councilman Al Sloan from St. Ignatius spoke "against liquidation and for a reorganization of the council by revising the method of selecting leadership." He wanted to see a "qualified businessman" run tribal assets. Kootenai Mary Antiste declared that "I'm getting out. I tell you — I'm tired of living like this — I tan, that's my living. All those people that got good jobs — they don't have to worry about their next meal, but I do. I know how to use a dollar and a penny and I'd make a good use of that money." Chuck Hunter of St. Ignatius thanked Morigeau for "waking people up," but said: "God have mercy on those who don't use [the money] right." Lucille Otter of Ronan pointed out the key issue: "Without a land-base we lose our identity." Gene Maillett of Dayton, a member of the Committee for Optional Withdrawal, argued that nobody was being forced to leave and claimed that "the Klamath Indians, who did not liquidate . . . are now getting better returns than ever." Salish Thomas "Bearhead" Swaney noted why elders like Mary Antiste might want to sell out: "The tribal council system is no longer valid. It is not helping the older Indians." However, he drew applause when he said: "Chief Joseph couldn't sell his land and I can't sell my land — not today — tomorrow — or any time."[42]

On February 5, the tribal council with a 7 to 0 vote approved Resolution 4005, "Removing E. W. Morigeau as tribal council delegate to the Montana Inter-Tribal Policy Board and the governing board of the Indian Community Action Program for calendar year 1971." The council cited Morigeau's "affiliation with the Committee for Optional Withdrawal [being] inconsistent with Tribal Council's Resolution 4002 . . . opposing liquidation and termination" as one of the reasons for the removal. Morigeau, Robert McCrea, and Al Sloan did not vote, in essence disapproving the resolution. Sloan and McCrea stated that the removal was "too personal."[43]

Morigeau did not let up, however. In late February he was in Spokane, Washington, speaking to the Confederated Salish and Kootenai enrollees living there. Morigeau claimed that 99 percent of the three hundred members present favored his plan. In Seattle, out of the 500 tribal members present, "100 per cent . . . were behind the plan," to "withdraw from the Flathead reservation and receive their pro-rata share of tribal assets." Out of three thousand petitions mailed to off-reservation tribal members, one thousand had been returned.[44] Be that as it may, the Salish and Kootenai constitution stated that 30 percent of eligible voters were needed to put an issue to a referendum, which did not take place at Flathead in 1971.

The March 6th tribal council meeting drew a record crowd of four hundred tribal members. On the agenda was the issue that got the Salish and Kootenai most excited — the upcoming payment of judgment money. The tribal council proposed 90 percent payout and 10 percent investment, while Morigeau and off-reservation members wanted 100 percent payment. The Committee for Optional Withdrawal read its resolution; in Article I they emphasized that "This is not a bill to terminate the Flathead Reservation." Article III stated that once a member chooses to withdraw and was paid his or her share, he/she "automatically Terminates himself from Tribal entity and also removes his status as wards of the Government." Finally, after the final roll, "no child born thereafter shall be eligible for enrollment." This, despite the committee's rhetoric, was termination. Lucille Otter pointed to the crowd and said: "it is the people — less than ¼ that want to terminate. All you have to do to get out of the Tribes is send an application into the Council and they will withdraw your name from the rolls." (This is, of course, without monetary compensation.) In the end, Morigeau's motion for 100 percent payout lost in the council 4 to 6, while the council's proposal for 90 percent payment carried 5 to 4 as Resolution 4027.[45]

In an April 2nd council meeting, Chairman Whitworth stated his support for H.R. 3333 and H.R. 3830 to provide "for disposition of judgments" for the congressional release of the payments from the U.S. Court of Claims case. The case concluded in a $22 million compensation, a very belated payment for lands lost due to the opening of the reservation to white settlement in 1910. This case, opened in 1951, also included a settlement from an erroneus survey of the southwest reservation boundary, minus attorneys' fees and ten percent going into tribal credit and other programs as ruled by law.[46] Morigeau wanted an option to take one's share of payment entirely in cash. Off-reservation Indians present demanded "the right to use our *per capita* share of this judgment money for our own purposes." The chairman's proposal for a $4,000 per capita distribution, the rest of the money going to investments, carried the day.[47]

Morigeau re-introduced his optional withdrawal proposal in 1984. According to the proposal, anyone wanting to leave tribal membership could do so and cash in his or her share of tribal assets. The renewed proposal rose from Morigeau's and many tribal members' frustrations regarding the tribes' business ventures, which had yet to turn into an all-out success. He and his associates wanted to "modernize the tribal government" by reducing the council from ten to five members and hiring a "badly needed manager." According to Morigeau, this would have saved the tribes $300,000 a year and would have trimmed down the "jealousy-ridden and secretive" council, and decreased the tribal government's incompetency.[48]

This time the organization proposing withdrawal was called a "$50,000 Club," after the amount of money the withdrawing members were to receive. The club, headed by Salish Fred Glover, was not proposing to "liquidate or terminate the Reservation, but [would] allow tribal members to withdraw their names from the per-capita rolls and receive a $50,000 cash settlement." Morigeau claimed this was a "move to preserve the Reservation for the young and the remaining members." The settlements were to be paid with money earned from timber sales. Morigeau believed that tribal members were worth more than $50,000, but the "withdrawing members" would sacrifice for the remaining members. The payout would have been made reality through a congressional bill that left treaty status intact, along with "aboriginal hunting and fishing." Morigeau believed that no other tribal income than timber sales needed to be touched, and that the tribes would save money in the long run, as only 269 members wished to withdraw (a figure which, compared to Morigeau's decade-old claims, seemed very low indeed). He claimed that because each tribal member's share of assets was worth $100,000, the tribes would save $13,450,000. In what time period the savings would take place, and on what evidence Morigeau based his figures was unclear. As expected, the tribal council and its new chairman Michael E. "Mickey" Pablo did not respond kindly to Morigeau's proposal. Morigeau especially had an issue with an unnamed councilman, possibly chairman Pablo, whom he accused of "openly criticizing tribal members," and of being responsible for "shut[ting] down two or three tribal enterprises at a cost of many jobs."[49]

Tribal elders interviewed in later years did not remember Morigeau kindly. Salish Thurman Trosper argued that Morigeau lost his council position due to fraudulent double-dipping on expenses. Trosper believed Morigeau pushed the issue for "greed," wanting to get his share of tribal assets.[50] Kootenai Al Hewankorn thought that Morigeau "pushed the issue because of the money." He believed Morigeau was about "lining his own pockets," and was supported by local ranchers who hoped to "get cheap leases." According to Hewankorn, Steve DeMers, who supported Morigeau's plans, was "white," although a tribal member. Kootenai Sadie Saloway believed 1971 was "closest we ever came to termination." She thought many people signed Morigeau's petitions "because of money and greed." However, they did not have "facts on what could be done after termination," so many "took their signatures back once they knew the reality." Kootenai Francis Auld argued that Morigeau used "assimilated Indians" to push his petition. Kootenai Adeline Mathias believed Morigeau "got money through some scheme," wanted "more money," and "didn't care about people."[51] As Saloway pointed out, a referendum never materialized because Morigeau and associates failed to find thirty percent of tribal members to sign and retain their signatures. This critique towards Morigeau does not, however, mean that the interviewed elders thought the tribal council acted appropriately in shutting down Morigeau. Trosper later proposed amending the tribal constitution to decrease the council's power because, according to him, the council "does not act [with] people's best interests in mind." [52]

Tribal Perception of the Possibility of Termination

In the late 1990s, the termination idea did not seem to be dead, as it on occasion came up from both within and outside the tribes, mostly from state and congressional politicians, even if the sporadic proposals always died out. By 1999, it seemed clear to tribal elders that even some Salish and Kootenai still wanted to see termination happen. The issue continued to play a dynamic role in tribal politics. Many off-reservation tribal members advocated termination thinking they would "get a lot of money." However, few on-reservation tribal members seemed to want termination, even if they expected it in the near future. The majority feared the potential loss of federal services, benefits, programs, and treaty rights. The threat clearly did exist, and tribal elder Dolly Linsebigler believed that the tribes had to be careful not to become terminated. Trosper was more pessimistic: He thought that the reservation would indeed be dissolved because "Congress will bring it out," as it has the ultimate authority, the plenary power.[53]

Another issue causing tension in the reservation between Indians and non-Indians was the tribes' 1995 proposal to take over the management of the 18,500 acre National Bison Range, carved from reservation lands in 1908. Since 2002 the tribes conducted on-going negotiations with the U.S. Department of Interior's Fish and Wildlife Service (USFWS) to take over the management of not just the Bison Range, but also the Ninepipe and Pablo National Wildlife Refuges (bird sanctuaries) in the central part of the reservation. In a March 11, 2003, meeting in Charlo, the tribes proposed to take over the management of these areas based on the 1994 Self-Governance Amendment to the 1975 Self-Determination Act. Local non-Indians took issue with the tribes' Indian-preference hiring policy, which they feared, would affect jobs at the refuges once the tribes took over. The Charlo meeting was organized by the Citizens Equal Rights Alliance, whose representatives argued that Indians did not pay taxes and received "free" healthcare and education, while emphasizing that this was "not a matter of white and Indian, but of equal rights."[54] To get management over the Bison Range, the tribes were required to prove that they had "historical, geographical and cultural ties" to the areas under federal management. Tribal Vice-Chairman Jami Hamel of Arlee noted that "The whole issue comes down to the sovereignty of our Tribes . . . They just don't want Indians to do it."[55]

Two more major meetings between the tribes and the locals regarding the issue took place, one in Ronan on May 15, 2003, and another in Missoula on June 3. Opinions, pro and con, pertaining to tribal management were presented in the meetings. One opponent claimed that "The American Indian does not have a history of caring management of any of their lands." Those who supported the proposal noted the tribes' "strong ties to the land and to the buffalo," and their other management successes.[56]

In 2004, the USFWS signed a two-year agreement with the tribes to co-manage the Bison Range. Tensions did not ease: by October 2006, the Fish and Wildlife Service ordered an outside investigation because non-Indian employees complained about deteriorating work conditions and tribal laxity in work performance since the agreement was signed.[57] Once the agreement expired, the tribes sought full management of the Bison Range, but the USFWS resisted until "'significant' personnel issues [were] resolved."[58] Thereafter tension between the sides escalated, so much so that both sides brought in security to ensure the safety of their workers. The USFWS stated that the decision not to continue temporary co-management was based on "poor performance, failure to correct it, and egregious personnel issues," in other words, incompetence in tribal management. Tribal Chairman James Steele, Jr., assured that the issue would not "stop here." Many non-Indian opponents of tribal management plans were thrilled by the USFWS decision.[59] Finally the two sides came to a management agreement, but kept mum on the details.[60] In this atmosphere of often-heated debate, it was not surprising that many tribal members were fearful of the return of termination; they perceived it as the ultimate goal of the anti-Indian rhetoric. Tensions with non-Indians increased internal debate about termination.

Termination by Dilution: Lineal Descent Proposal

Another reoccurrence of the termination paradigm arose from an effort to amend the tribal constitution to reform tribal government in the end of the 1990s and, after its failure, the subsequent proposal to expand tribal enrollment. Ever since the adoption of the new constitution in 1935, tribal members have generally been unhappy with the council's nearly unchecked power and the tribal enrollment rules.[61] These issues came into conflict in the period between 1999 and 2003 in a way that reminded many tribal members of the federal attempts at termination during the 1950s. They believed that diluting tribal blood through expanded enrollment might open the door for renewed local and state calls for termination leading to federal efforts at abolishing tribal status and services. After all, the tribes had amended their constitution twice in the 1950s to make enrollment more strict and to thereby defeat termination by appearing more "Indian."

Enrollment eligibility had been a very divisive issue for the Salish and Kootenai. Intermarriages were common and the matter of Indian descent had become increasingly complicated, with many split families, within which some members were, while others were not, eligible for tribal membership. Tribal Resolution 1072 of February 2, 1960, was approved in a referendum. It officially amended Article II of the constitution and established current enrollment requirements. A person must be "a natural child" of an enrolled member, be "¼ or more Salish or Kootenai blood," and "not enrolled in another reservation." These requirements were not retroactive and therefore did not take away membership from now ineligible Indians already enrolled. Nevertheless, the tribal council could adopt members of minimum one eighth Indian blood with the secretary of the interior's approval. Tribal membership could be lost due to resignation, to "enrollment with another tribe," to "establishing a legal residence in a foreign country," or "upon proof of lack of eligibility for enrollment."[62]

In the late 1990s, there were two arguments which divided the tribes: whether to broaden the membership base to include Indians less than one quarter Salish or Kootenai blood or to keep membership standards strict in order to preserve tribal identity. Salish Doug Allard was one of those who favored loosening the membership criteria. "We are running out of Indians," he observed. Indeed the tribal membership was predicted to drop from near 7,000 to 5,000 by 2026.[63]

A thirty-two-member constitutional review committee, established in January 1996 and chaired by Allard, became a sounding board for the enrollment debate. The final push for establishing the committee came when the tribal council, especially its chairman, Mickey Pablo, reversed a tribal judge's ruling by giving clemency to a tribal member convicted of an offense. Many tribal members questioned whether a true separation of powers therefore existed in the tribal government. The council's action, after all, was legitimate: the tribal constitution left the "ultimate authority" to the council. The committee was expected to suggest cutting the tribal council's supreme power and to make it more accountable to the tribal membership by amending the tribal constitution in a way that would guarantee real separation of powers. The council was to become reduced to a solely legislative body, and an executive director was to be elected to be in charge of the tribal budget.[64] Thurman Trosper, a member of the committee, noted that the council lacked management skills and had squandered opportunities; nepotism was rampant. Trosper acknowledged that the council would not give up its powers without a fight, but the "council's politicking has to be overcome." He charged that the tribal constitution was inadequate because the legal structure to force the tribal council to delegate power was missing, thereby confirming the deficiencies in the BIA-written constitution.[65]

Trosper's fears of difficulties in trying to change the tribal constitution came true: the constitutional review committee failed to force a change, and by 2000 Trosper and others had decided to try another method to deal with the rampant problems. This was an effort to expand tribal membership to all lineal descendants. This proposal stirred a major hornets' nest among tribal members.

Split families, the fact that some family members were enrolled while others were not, obviously was, and still remains, a major problem. Noel Pichette, a Salish who was a councilman from 1975 to 1983 and a member of the constitutional review committee, acknowledged this in 1999. He opposed the lineal descent idea, but noted how "many elders want their non-members in [the] family enrolled." Dolly Linsebigler was concerned about intermarriages, and worried that if the tribes didn't do anything "there'll be no more Indians." She proposed changing the enrollment rules to allow those minimum of one quarter of "any Indian blood [to] qualify as long as [they were] not enrolled in another Tribe." Thurman Trosper pointed out the other significant issue in the matter: new members would cut into the $1,200 annual per capita payments.[66]

Others advocated keeping tribal membership criteria in its present form or wanted even further restrictions. Once again, the argument revolved around blood-quantum and perceived Indian identity or lack of it. The rhetoric got quite contentious at times, as exemplified by Augustine Mathias, an elderly Kootenai from Elmo: "People wake up before they pull another fast one on us. I'm talking about letting a bunch more white people on the rolls. They have pushed us to the edge of cultural extinction as it is." He continued: "it's just another attempt by greedy whites to gain more control over our resources . . . They will take what little we have for their own economic gain." He continued with what this debate ultimately hinged on: "who has 95 percent of the good paying jobs in the tribal system? In my opinion, diluting the blood even more with white blood will not benefit the Indians who are already struggling to survive."[67] One splinter group in the reservation, calling themselves "¼ th for Reform Movement," wanted to limit tribal membership to a minimum of one quarter Salish or Kootenai without any possibility for the council to make exceptions.[68]

In the fall of 2000 the Kootenai Tribe presented an enrollment ordinance to the tribal council, proposing that the Kootenai would thereafter "assume the exclusive responsibilities for tribal enrollment of Kootenai Indians." The tribes' legal department shot down this idea of a separate Kootenai enrollment board because the tribal constitution did not recognize any Kootenai Tribe, only the Confederated Salish and Kootenai Tribes, and because the constitution gave all authority on decisions regarding enrollment to the tribal council.[69] New council chairman Fred Matt sent a letter to the Kootenai that same day, applauding their efforts "to stem the loss of culture and to secure the protection of Tribal identity for the future survival of the Tribes." He, however, could not approve the proposed changes in the enrollment procedures, as he deemed them "illegal" and inviting inequality in membership procedures if approved. He suggested that all efforts to propose ways to improve cultural survival to be presented to the council "for review and possible implementation," a method which the Kootenai argued led nowhere.[70]

Some Kootenai then created a Flathead Indian Reservation Defense Organization (FIRDO). This group got deeply involved in the lineal descent referendum. They opposed it and saw it as a way to open the door for termination. The proposal's proponents, however, gained enough signatures to get it to a referendum vote, which took place on January 18, 2003.

The tribes hired a consultant, Deward Walker, to investigate possible enrollment scenarios. In his December 2002 report Walker concluded that if no changes in enrollment were made, the tribal enrollment would drop from 6,953 in 2001 to 6,900 by 2010 and to 6,400 by 2020. If the tribes changed their enrollment criteria to include "blood of other tribes for currently enrolled tribal members thereby affecting their descendants' blood quantum," enrollment would increase to 7,690 by 2005, but would then drop to 7,290 by 2020. Finally, if the lineal descent proposal were adopted, the tribes would have 17,159 members by 2010 and 24,107 by 2025, argued Walker who based his figures on an annual growth rate of 2.4 percent.[71]

By using these potentially tendentious figures, FIRDO asked for a halt or delay on the referendum fearing that their members would "become a small minority on the reservation and [would] lose their voice in government affairs." They were also concerned about benefits being "watered down" should the amendment pass. U.S. District Court Judge Donald Molloy refused to interfere "in the political process of the sovereign tribal government." Enrolled members who turned eighteen by the election day and had resided on the reservation for at least a year prior could vote; eligible voters totaled 3,173.[72]

Tribal members started an intense debate on the proposal in the days leading to the election. One wrote that tribal enrollment criteria was a result of federal threats to take away "medical, educational and welfare assistance," that is, termination. He considered lineal descent as a way to "restore membership" to what the chiefs had intended when they accepted the treaty. Another blamed the tribal council for presenting just the negatives about increased membership. She questioned the need to "perpetuate Indian blood identification through a mathematical fraction imposed by the United States" and believed added tribal members would increase the pool for tribal jobs, not add any workload to law and order, and make membership criteria more equal.[73]

Jacqueline Britton, a tribal member from Sacramento, California, supported the amendment because "By insisting on blood quantum, you will eventually lose many, many people who are Salish in their lives as well as in their hearts." Her children could not be enrolled, but "None of them want[ed] tribal money." They simply wanted "acknowledgment" of being Salish, she claimed. Lillian Hartung argued that the council was threatening people with losing their benefits, just like the U.S. government had done earlier through some "extortion method," if they approved added members.[74] Vera Rosengren claimed that the council's stand against the amendment was "scare tactics and propaganda." She thought that no matter where one lived, they were "still Flathead," so the entire membership should be entitled to vote. Her children knew of "their heritage and cannot claim it because of the current 'tribal constitution.'" Nancy Brown Vaughn advocated the amendment noting how a "majority" of the tribes' ninety-five councilmen since 1935 "have been less than full blood and several were even less than ¼ degree." She reminded her readers that "most of us share the idea that our children are our most important resource for the future."[75]

In contrast with these letters promoting the amendment, many tribal members adamantly opposed it; the tribes therefore were seriously divided. Susan Dowdall said she was "proud" to be a full blood and stated that the council waited too long to take a stand against the amendment. Referring to the national deficit, she argued that no additional money could be expected from the federal government, and therefore the burden of thousands of additional members would be too much for the tribes to bear. Cainan Monroe noted that, first of all, the "enrollment system was designed to destroy the native population." He was afraid that if the lineal descent proposal were adopted, "then you can expect termination of the reservation and the stripping of our identity to follow soon after." The amendment proposal reminded him strongly of termination of the 1950s: "when people start being enrolled on the basis of nothing more than a story . . . eventually it will lead the U.S. Government . . . to ask the question of 'who is really an Indian?' . . . Then the government has no reason to classify natives as a separate entity, or sovereign nations . . . we are a target for the U.S. Government, mainly for our resources, and minerals." He thought the lineal descent issue was a "setup" to abolish the tribes and proposed enrolling people with "other native blood," a proposal which had quite a bit support on the reservation. Finally, he concluded how "Creating disputes amongst ourselves such as the enrollment issue leaves us vulnerable to outside political attack."[76] Here he pointed out an important dichotomy: The tribes perceived that their internal divisions had made it easier for the federal, state, and local governments to divide and conquer, and thereby subjugate and colonialize indigenous peoples. Tribal traditions had never promoted complete unity, which had made it hard for the tribal governments to show decisiveness.

On the eve of the January 16th election, chairman Matt warned the tribal membership that "the lineal descendancy amendment would have serious and detrimental impacts on our Tribe . . . The Salish-Kootenai would become the new Cherokees of the West, where even a tiny fraction of Indian blood would qualify one for enrollment."[77] However, the Split Family Support Group (SFSG) that pushed for the referendum believed that federal funding for many services would increase, and "Many other programs, entitlements and privileges of tribal membership could continue without significant changes if the Tribal Council managed resources wisely and governed effectively."[78]

During the election, 2,549 Salish and Kootenai out of the eligible 3,173 voted in eight polling places in Indian community centers of Arlee, Dixon, Elmo-Dayton, Hot Springs, Pablo,

Polson, Ronan, and St. Ignatius. Exactly 2,032 opposed the proposal while 450 approved it with the remaining 67 votes not
counting. Therefore 80 percent of the eligible voted, an unusually
high turnout; a very divisive issue drew people to polling places.
Elmo, the Kootenai community and a "stronghold" of FIRDO
and "cultural traditionals," voted in the 80 percent range, "the
most votes we've ever had."[79]

The SFSG admitted defeat and stated that the election
"closed the door for tribal identification of our unenrolled descendants." Thurman Trosper supported the amendment from
a frustration to get the constitutional review committee to
succeed, and because "tribal members fail to understand and ap-
preciate that with the current one quarter degree requirement for
membership, it ultimately spells the death knell of the tribes."
He also criticized the tribal council for not helping SFSG's earlier effort, in 2000, to amend the tribal constitution to allow
enrollment of siblings of members, which the BIA rejected on
technical grounds.[80] Doug Allard thought that the defeat of the
amendment was "the stupidest damn thing that ever happened,"
and claimed that people were afraid for their $1,200 per capita
payments.[81]

Because of the issue's divisive nature, chairman Matt called
for tribal unity after the election, admitting that "this election
definitely strained the fabric of our tribal community."[82] To this
observer, unfortunately, it appeared that this unity may be very
hard to achieve. It was clear that something needed to be done to
tribal enrollment practices.

Opposition to lineal descent was much more pronounced
at a more traditional Kootenai district in the northern part of
the reservation than in a more business-astute Salish community,
where even many elders, such as Trosper and Allard, advocated
the change. Most certainly they did not advocate termination,
although some saw the proposal as a move to that direction.
Kootenai Ignace Couture saw the issue in terms of some "people

trying to get back in because living [is] getting more expensive."
He believed that passing the referendum "would have put an
economic squeeze on all." While the split family advocates were
saying "that you would get more money from [federal] government, government could bring up the issue of termination as
a result." He credited the tribal council for handling the issue
well, although three council members promoted lineal descent.
He put the whole matter into historical perspective by noting
how the "split family deal" started in the 1950s when the tribes
changed their enrollment criteria for fear of termination.[83]

Al Hewankorn agreed with Couture. He noted how the
termination issue disappeared with E. W. Morigeau, who died
in 1990, but reappeared with the lineal descent proposal. He
believed that the "federal government would have jumped in
to argue for termination." Sadie Saloway noted that only 450
people voted for lineal descent while a thousand signatures were
needed to bring the issue to a referendum. She concluded that
many who supported the idea did so because they had family
members who were unenrolled, but they voted against it "because [they] realized what it would do." She stated that "we were
very afraid" that the amendment might pass, but when it did not,
"faith comes back to your people." In contrast with Couture, Saloway did not think the council handled the matter well, because
there are "many non-Indians on the council."[84]

Francis Auld noted how the lineal descent issue "brought
up the extremists from both sides." He saw the tribal constitution
as the issue that divided the tribes. He credited people's "sense"
for defeating the proposal. Adeline Mathias believed that lineal
descent would bring "faster termination" than anything, because
it would quickly dilute Indianness of tribal members.[85] Mathias'
granddaughter Lois Friedlander, a FIRDO activist, pointed out
how the council got involved in the matter only when FIRDO
hired an attorney "to let people know what would happen."
She agreed with Saloway in that many of those who signed a

referendum petition voted against the proposal because they "found out what it means." She noted how termination was a valid threat nationally by referring to Senate Bill 1721, introduced by retiring Senator Ben Nighthorse Campbell (R-CO) in 2004, which would have reduced the official federal blood-quantum three points below one quarter to "allow keeping trust status on lands for lineal descendants."[86]

The last issue regarding lineal descent concerned the three tribal council members who supported the amendment. In the January 28, 2003, council meeting, Wilbert Michel, president of FIRDO, asked Maggie Goode (Hot Springs), Joel Clairmont (Polson), and Denny Orr (Arlee) if "they believe[d] they [were] working in the best interest of the Indian people." They believed they were. Michel asked them to "step down from the council." Goode stated that she "was elected to represent all the people," who had a "constitutional right for a fair secretarial election" (referendum). Clairmont and Orr agreed, and all hoped to move on. Tribal member Pat Pierre requested that the "council move forward with the proposal for the inclusion of other Indian bloods for enrollment criteria." Tribal member Junior Caye requested a motion to remove Goode, Orr, and Clairmont from the council, but vice-chair Jami Hamel insisted a proper procedure be followed. Finally the council agreed to "obtain a legal review on the process to remove a tribal council member from office" with a 9 to 0 vote, with Goode abstaining.[87]

FIRDO later clarified that their request to remove the three councilmen was based on their violation of tribal constitution and code of conduct. Chairman Matt noted that councilmen can be removed only "if they are proven guilty of improper conduct or gross neglect of duty." Neither charge applied here and the councilmen kept their seats.[88] However, Goode and Orr lost their seats in the November 2003 council elections while Clairmont lost his seat in 2004.

Conclusion

The policy to terminate Indian reservations started in the United States Congress during World War II. For the conservative coalition of southern Democrats and northern Republicans, the New Deal Indian policy and the Indian Reorganization Act of 1934 appeared to further tie Indians onto reservations instead of pushing them to assimilate and become a part of mainstream America. Restrictions placed on Indian ownership of property seemed a hindrance to their "freedom" and assimilation. Besides giving Indians their "freedom," the congressional mood during and immediately after the war required cutbacks in the New Deal federal programs and government. Indian affairs seemed a suitable target.

Those tribes that had abundant reservation resources and a tribal population that had long mixed with whites were easily labeled as ready subjects to assume responsibility for their own affairs. These tribes faced a paradox: Since the mid-nineteenth-century the federal government had attempted to settle tribes onto reservations and make farmers out of their members. Now those who had best adapted to this policy were to lose their lands. The Confederated Salish and Kootenai Tribes (CSKT) were one of these tribes.

The CSKT were the first Indian nation to adopt the Indian Reorganization Act, and they ratified a constitution and bylaws the following year. The constitution gave the ten-member tribal council a large authority over tribal members subject to the approval of secretary of the interior. Over the years the tribal council has been criticized for not being representative of the entire tribal membership, for being the voice of the Bureau of Indian Affairs (BIA), and for not being competent in its financial dealings. Despite the criticism, the strength of the CSKT tribal council enabled it to oppose the efforts of Congress and the BIA to terminate the Flathead Indian Reservation in the 1950s. Tribal leaders based their key arguments on the inviolability of treaty rights and on the importance of keeping tribal lands in trust. Termination would have been a violation of the 1855 treaty and would have led to hardship and poverty for tribal members.

Tribal opposition aroused the State of Montana to fear the negative consequences of termination in the form of increased welfare and health costs, which the added tax base would not have covered. Tribal opposition also raised sympathy from Montana's U.S. Senators, James Murray and Mike Mansfield, and Representative Lee Metcalf. While the three M's in principle agreed with the philosophy of termination, they argued that the timing was not right and the schedule to end federal responsibility for reservation affairs was too fast. The CSKT were not ready for termination.

Tribal, state, and congressional opposition factored in the defeat of termination at Flathead. If one or all of these factors had been missing, the reservation would likely have been terminated, as happened in the cases of the Klamath, the Menominee, and the Uintah-Ouray Reservations. The Klamaths and the Menominees had ample resources and were divided over the issue of withdrawal of federal supervision. They did not have the support of their states' congressional delegations. While the Uintah-Ouray Reservation contained few resources, the Uintah and Ute tribes were divided and their state's U.S. Senator Arthur Watkins was determined to make them an example of termination.

While the Salish and Kootenai avoided termination, the victory came with a price. The interests of those tribal members who favored termination and liquidation of tribal assets were sacrificed. These individuals did not have much influence in tribal affairs and relatively little support among the tribal members, but they became even more alienated from tribal affairs as the result of the failed liquidation effort. Had the Salish and Kootenai had deeper internal divisions in the 1950s they might well have lost their reservation. In the early 1970s tribal members debated the issues of liquidation of tribal assets and optional withdrawal from the tribe, causing the tribal council to lose its unity on the matter. A vast majority of tribal members still disliked liquidation. By this time Congress favored self-determination in Indian affairs, so the advocates of liquidation did not have many supporters in the nation's capitol.

The threat of termination did not disappear, however, not at Flathead nor nationally. In the early 2000s, with the debate over a proposed amendment to the tribal constitution and a 2003 referendum on changing tribal enrollment rules to linear descent, the issue raised considerable debate. Many Salish and Kootenai felt that expanding enrollment to additional members would open the door to congressional efforts to terminate the reservation. The debate was intense, and at times personal. It slowly abated after the referendum to change enrollment rules was defeated. In this, the Salish and Kootenai were not alone. For example, the Colville Indian Reservation in Washington State went through a similar debate. Laurie Arnold in *Bartering with the Bones of Their Dead: The Colville Confederated Tribes and Termination* tells the story about how the tribal debate over termination lasted well beyond the discussion in Congress. As at Flathead, the Colville Reservation debate was complex, intense, and often personal, but it ended in the defeat of termination advocates.[1] One of the ironies of the debate over termination on the Flathead Reservation was that the threat made the tribes stronger and fostered a growing commitment among tribal members to defend and preserve the tribes, their culture, and ways of life.

Notes

Abbreviations Used in Footnotes

Burgess Papers — Lorena M. Burgess Papers, MS 566, K. Ross Toole Archives, Mansfield Library, University of Montana, Missoula.

CSKT Minutes — Tribal Council Minutes, Confederated Salish and Kootenai Tribes, Pablo, Montana.

FH Termination Hearings — *Termination of Federal Supervision Over Certain Tribes of Indians,* Joint Hearings Before the Subcommittees of the Committees on Interior and Insular Affairs, 83rd Congress, 2d Session, 1954, Part 7, Flathead.

In the Name — Robert Bigart and Clarence Woodcock, eds., *In the Name of the Salish & Kootenai Nation: The 1855 Hell Gate Treaty and the Origin of the Flathead Indian Reservation* (Pablo, Mont.: Salish Kootenai College Press, 1996). Among other things the book includes Albert J. Partoll, ed., "Official Proceedings of the Hell Gate Treaty Council," pages 19-65; John C. Ewers, "Gustavus Sohon's Portraits of Flathead and Pend d'Oreille Indians, 1854," pages 67-120; and Robert Ignatius Burns, S.J., "A Jesuit at the Hell Gate Treaty of 1855," pages 121-148.

Metcalf Papers — Lee Metcalf Papers, Collection No. 172, Montana Historical Society Archives, Helena.

Murray Papers — James E. Murray Papers, MS 91, K. Ross Toole Archives, Mansfield Library, University of Montana, Missoula.

* * * * * *

Chapter 1

1. Quoted in Merrill G. Burlingame, "Historical Report Concerning Lands Ceded to the United States Government by the Flathead, Pend d'Oreille and Kutenai Indians by the Treaty of 1855," David Agee Horr, comp. and ed., *Interior Salish and Eastern Washington Indians II*, American Indian Ethnohistory Series: Indians of the Northwest, Vol. II (New York: Garland Publishing, 1974), 198-207.

2. *In the Name*, 1; also Albert J. Partoll, "Official Proceedings of the Hell Gate Treaty Council," *In the Name*, 19, 24; and Robert Ignatius Burns, S.J., "A Jesuit at the Hell Gate Treaty of 1855," *In the Name*, 123-124.

3. For bibliographic reference to and portraits of the various Salish leaders of 1855, see John C. Ewers, "Gustavus Sohon's Portraits of Flathead and Pend d'Oreille Indians, 1854," *In the Name*, 67-120.

4. Red Wolf quote *In the Name*, 29.

5. *In the Name*, 28-29, 39, 42.

6. *In the Name*, 49.

7. Isaac I. Stevens, Governor and Superintendent of Indian Affairs, Washington Territory to George W. Manypenny, Commissioner of Indian Affairs, July 16, 1855, *In the Name*, 64. Stevens estimated the numbers of the three tribes as: 450 Flatheads, 350 Kootenai, and 600 Upper Pend Oreilles, In the Name, 62.

8. *In the Name*, 2; John Fahey, *The Flathead Indians* (Norman: University of Oklahoma Press, 1974), xii, 102, 109.

9. *In the Name*, 2, 9-14.

10. *In the Name*, 14-15.

11. Burton M. Smith, "The Politics of Allotment: The Flathead Indian Reservation as a Test Case," *Pacific Northwest Quarterly,* 70 (No. 3, July 1979): 132, 139; Donald L. Parman, *Indians and the American West in the Twentieth Century* (Bloomington: Indiana University Press, 1994), 14-16.

12. Fahey, *Flathead Indians*, 227-229.

13. Ibid., 257, 264, 279; Editorial, *Missoulian*, Dec. 24, 1903, quoted in Smith, "Politics of Allotment," 132-133; Parman, *Indians and American West*, 15.

14. Smith, "Politics of Allotment," 133-136; Fahey, *Flathead Indians*, 272; Parman, *Indians and American West*, 15.

15. Charlo quote from transcript of the Council Meeting at St. Ignatius, Jan. 3-4, 1901, quoted in Smith, "Politics of Allotment," 136-138.

16. Smith, "Politics of Allotment," 137; Fahey, *Flathead Indians*, 246, 279; Parman, *Indians and American West*, 16.

17. Ronald Lloyd Trosper, "The Economic Impact of the Allotment Policy on the Flathead Indian Reservation" (Ph.D. dissertation, Harvard University, 1974), 6; Quote from Charles McDonald taped interview transcript, no date, Montana Historical Society Archives, OH 262, Tape I, side B, Tape III, side B.

18. Terry Anderson, *Sovereign Nations or Reservations?: An Economic History of American Indians* (San Francisco: Pacific Research Institute for Public Policy, 1995), 122.

19. Charles Thomas Brockmann, "The Modern Social and Economic Organization of the Flathead Reservation" (Ph.D. dissertation, University of Oregon, 1968), 1, 7, 59.

20. Noel Pichette interview with author, Salish Longhouse, St. Ignatius, Montana, June 11, 1999.

21. Fahey, *Flathead Indians*, 281-299; Diane L. Krahe, "A Confluence of Sovereignty and Conformity: The Mission Mountains Tribal Wilderness" (MA thesis, University of Montana, 1995), 26-27.

22. [Supervisor John H. Holst,] "Some Observations on the Former Flathead Reservation," April 3, 1943, 4, 11, Desk Files, Supt. C. C. Wright, Box 4, Flathead Agency Papers, 8NS-075-96-322, Record Group 75, National Archives Rocky Mountain Region, Denver. This report by Supervisor Holst was very sympathetic toward termination.

23. Testimony of Lorena Burgess, *FH Termination Hearings*, 1009. Burgess no doubt used Holst's report to support her argument, but even she would disagree with Holst's statement that: "It is the height of folly to continue to try to deal with the problems involved in the Flathead case on the basis of old treaties which were merely a hypothecation of plans to be developed later," Holst report, 10, National Archives, Denver.

24. John Collier, *From Every Zenith: A Memoir and Some Essays on Life and Thought* (Denver: Sage Books, 1963), 173.

25. *Congressional Record*, Senate, 73rd Congress, 2d session, June 12, 1934, 11123.

26. *Congressional Record*, House, 73rd Congress, 2d session, June 15, 1934, 11731.

27. "Roosevelt Speaks for Indians' Rights," *New York Times*, April 29, 1934, 34.

28. "The Indian Reorganization Act (Wheeler-Howard Act), 1934," Albert Hurtado and Peter Iverson, eds., *Major Problems in American Indian History*. Second Edition (Boston: Houghton-Mifflin, 2001), 388-391.

29. Russel Lawrence Barsh and James Youngblood Henderson, *The Road: Indian Tribes and Political Liberty* (Berkeley: University of California Press, 1980), 101-105.

30. James S. Olson and Raymond Wilson, *Native Americans in the Twentieth Century* (Provo: Brigham Young University Press, 1984), 24.

31. D'Arcy McNickle, "The Indian New Deal as Mirror of the Future," Hurtado and Iverson, eds., *Major Problems*, 411-413.

32. Collier, *From Every Zenith*, 203.

33. Robert Hecht, *Oliver La Farge and the American Indian: A Biography* (Metuchen, N.J.: Scarecrow Press, 1991), 89.

34. "Indians' New Deal Brings on a Clash," *New York Times*, March 14, 1937, 16; "Two Camps Form over Indian Law," *New York Times*, March 28, 1937, 63.

35. Lawrence Kelly, "The Indian Reorganization Act: The Dream and the Reality," *Pacific Historical Review*, 44 (No. 3, Aug. 1975): 296, 298; Kenneth R. Philp, *John Collier's Crusade for Indian Reform 1920-1954* (Tucson: University of Arizona Press, 1977), 138, 160-161; Graham D. Taylor, "The Tribal Alternative to Bureaucracy: The Indian's New Deal, 1933-1945," *Journal of the West*, 13 (No. 1, Jan. 1974): 136.

36. "Four Years of Self-Government Completed by Confederated Selish, Kootenai Tribes," *The Daily Missoulian*, Nov. 12, 1939, ed. section, 6.

37. L. W. Shotwell, Superintendent, Flathead Agency, Montana, "End of an Era — Beginning of a New?" *Indians at Work*, 3 (Reorganization Number, 1936), 29-30.

38. Flathead Culture Committee, *A Brief History of the Flathead Tribes* (St. Ignatius: Flathead Culture Committee, 1979), 4.

39. Constitution and Bylaws of the Confederated Salish and Kootenai Tribes of the Flathead Reservation, Article III, Box 66, Record Group 75, National Archives, Denver. Martin Charlo was chief Charlo's son.

40. James J. Lopach, "The Anomaly of Judicial Activism in Indian Country," *American Indian Culture and Research Journal*, 21 (No. 2, 1997): 91; Thurman Trosper interview with author, Trosper's home, Ronan, Montana, June 12, 1999; Constitution and Bylaws, Article VI, National Archives, Denver.

41. Trosper interview; also see Holst report, 17, National Archives, Denver.

42. Charles McDonald taped interview, passim, Montana Historical Society; also see Walter W. McDonald to Jim Cannon, Area Director, Bureau of Indian Affairs, Oct. 1, 1962, 5, Folder 4, Box 230, Lee Metcalf Papers.

43. James J. Lopach, Margery Hunter Brown, and Richmond L. Clow, *Tribal Government Today: Politics on Montana Indian Reservations*. Revised edition (Niwot: University Press of Colorado, 1998), 166.

44. Constitution and Bylaws, Article VIII, National Archives, Denver; Shotwell, "End of an Era," 30. By an order of Feb. 13, 1936, Secretary of the Interior restored 192,000 acres remaining of lands previously opened to settlement to the tribe, *FH Termination Hearings*, 779.

45. Lopach, Brown and Clow, *Tribal Government Today*, 165; Lopach, "Anomaly of Judicial Activism," 92.

46. Constitution and Bylaws, passim, National Archives, Denver.

47. Enrollment Correspondence, Box 331, Record Group 75, National Archives, Denver; Constitution and Bylaws, Article II, National Archives, Denver.

48. Donald L. Fixico, *Termination and Relocation: Federal Indian Policy, 1945-1960* (Albuquerque: University of New Mexico Press, 1986), 15-17.

49. *Survey of Conditions among the Indians of the United States: Analysis of the Statement of the Commissioner of Indian Affairs in Justification of Appropriations for 1944, and the Liquidation of the Indian Bureau*, Senate Report No. 310, 78th Congress, 1st session, June 11, 1943, serial 10756, 8-22.

50. S. Lyman Tyler, *Indian Affairs: A Study of the Changes in Policy of the United States toward Indians* (Provo: Institute of American Indian Studies, Brigham Young University, 1964), 96.

51. *Investigate Indian Affairs*, Hearings before the Committee on Indian Affairs, House, 78th Congress, 1st and 2d sessions, 1943-1944, part 1, 16.

52. Alison Bernstein, *American Indians and World War II: Toward a New Era in Indian Affairs* (Norman: University of Oklahoma Press, 1991), 109; Laurence Hauptman, *The Iroquois Struggle for Survival: World War II to Red Power* (Syracuse: Syracuse University Press, 1986), 11.

53. *An Investigation to Determine Whether the Changed Status of the Indian Requires a Revision of Laws and Regulations Affecting the American Indian,* A Report of the Select Committee to Investigate Indian Affairs and Conditions in the United States, House Report No. 2091, 78th Cong., 2d Sess., 1944, serial 10848, 2-16.

54. *Repealing the So-Called Wheeler-Howard Act,* Senate Report No. 1031, 78th Congress, 2d session, June 22, 1944, serial 10842, 1-16.

55. Lewis Meriam and associates, *The Problem of Indian Administration: Institute for Government Research Studies in Administration* (Baltimore: Johns Hopkins Press, 1928), 19, 48.

56. Report of Commissioner of Indian Affairs John Collier, 1934, Wilcomb E. Washburn, ed., *The American Indian and the United States: A Documentary History,* Volume II (New York: Random House, 1973), 914.

57. *Congressional Record,* House, 75th Congress, 1st session, June 23rd, 1937, 6241-6242.

58. Harvey D. Rosenthal, *Their Day in Court: A History of the Indian Claims Commission* (New York: Garland Publishing, 1990), 169-170, 245-246; also see Donald McCoy and Richard Ruetten, *Quest and Response: Minority Rights and the Truman Administration* (Lawrence: The University Press of Kansas, 1973), 42; Representative Karl Mundt, *Congressional Record,* House, 79th Congress, 2nd session, May 20, 1946, 5315-5316; Sandra C. Danforth, "Repaying Historical Debts: The Indian Claims Commission," *North Dakota Law Review,* 49 (No. 2, Winter 1973): 364-366.

59. Imre Sutton, "Prolegomena," Imre Sutton, ed., *Irredeemable America: The Indians' Estate and Land Claims* (Albuquerque: University of New Mexico Press, 1985), 9.

60. Fixico, *Termination and Relocation,* 30.

61. Rosenthal, *Their Day in Court,* 178-179.

62. Nancy Oestreich Lurie, "The Indian Claims Commission," *The Annals of the American Academy of Political and Social Science,* 436 (American Indians Today, March 1978): 100-102; United States Indian Claims Commission, *United States Indian Claims Commission: Final Report* (Washington, D.C.: Government Printing Office, 1979), 125.

63. *Report of Proceedings: Dillon S. Myer of Ohio to be Commissioner of Indian Affairs,* Hearing held before Committee on Interior and Insular Affairs, Senate, 81st Congress, 2d session, April 10, 1950, 4.

64. Larry J. Hasse, "Termination and Assimilation: Federal Indian Policy, 1943 to 1961," (Ph.D. dissertation, Washington State University, 1974), DAI 7416367, 110-112; Fixico, *Termination and Relocation,* 64-66; Kenneth R.

Philp, *Termination Revisited: American Indians on the Trail to Self-Determination, 1933-1953* (Lincoln: University of Nebraska Press, 1999), 87-90; Richard Drinnon, *Keeper of Concentration Camps: Dillon S. Myer and American Racism* (Berkeley: University of California Press, 1987), 163-168.

65. Dillon S. Myer, "Indian Administration: Problems and Goals," *Social Service Review,* 27 (No.2, June 1953): 196-197; Memorandum from the Commissioner of the Bureau of Indian Affairs to all Bureau Officials, August 5, 1952, reprinted in *House Report No. 2503*, 82nd Cong, 2d Sess, 1953, serial 11582, 3.

66. Myer, "Indian Administration," 198-200.

67. Memorandum from the Commissioner to Bureau Officials, *House Report No. 2503*, 3; Frederick J. Stefon, "The Irony of Termination: 1943-1958," *Indian Historian,* 11 (No. 3, Summer 1978): 7.

68. *Report of Proceedings*, 45-48.

69. Fixico, *Termination and Relocation*, 46; Hasse, "Termination and Assimilation," 71; Larry Burt, *Tribalism in Crisis: Federal Indian Policy, 1953-1961* (Albuquerque: University of New Mexico Press, 1982), 21.

70. McCoy and Ruetten, *Quest and Response*, 147, 305; Fixico, *Termination and Relocation*, 93.

71. Arthur V. Watkins, "Termination of Federal Supervision: The Removal of Restrictions over Indian Property and Person," *The Annals of the American Academy of Political and Social Science,* 311 (May 1957): 48.

72. Quote in *Congressional Record*, Senate, 83rd Congress, 1st session, July 24, 1953, 9743; Carolyn Grattan-Aiello, "Senator Arthur V. Watkins and the Termination of Utah's Southern Paiute Indians," *Utah Historical Quarterly,* 63 (No. 3, Summer 1995): 269, 272, 282; R. Warren Metcalf, "Arthur V. Watkins and the Indians of Utah: A Study of Federal Termination Policy" (Ph.D. dissertation, Arizona State University, 1995), DAI 9611697, iii, 22-23, 41-42.

73. Butler quote in *Congressional Record*, Senate, 81st Congress, 1st session, Oct. 7, 1949, 14119; Burt, *Tribalism in Crisis*, 4-5.

74. Steven Schulte, "Removing the Yoke of Government: E. Y. Berry and the Origins of Indian Termination Policy," *South Dakota History,* 14 (No. 1, Spring 1984): 49-61.

75. Address of Governor John W. Bonner before the Governors Conference on Indian Affairs at Houston, Texas, July 2, 1952, 5, Folder 19, Box 2, Burgess Papers.

76. "15 States United to Aid the Indians," *New York Times*, May 21, 1950, 67; Gladwin Hill, "9 States Urge U.S. Yield All 'Gas' Tax," *New York Times,* Dec. 10, 1952, 25; Philp, *Termination Revisited*, 95.

77. "Objectives of the Governors' Interstate Council on Indian Affairs," 1-2, Folder 15, Box 2, Burgess Papers.

78. Nicholas Peroff, *Menominee DRUMS: Tribal Termination and Restoration, 1954-1974* (Norman: University of Oklahoma Press, 1982), 61-62; Tyler, *Indian Affairs*, 5-7; S. Lyman Tyler, *A History of Indian Policy* (Washington, D.C: U.S. Department of the Interior, Bureau of Indian Affairs, 1973), 8.

79. House Concurrent Resolution 108, 83rd Congress, 1st session, adopted Aug. 1, 1953, printed in *House Report No. 2680: With Respect to the House Resolution Authorizing the Committee of Interior and Insular Affairs to Conduct an Investigation of the Bureau of Indian Affairs*, 83rd Congress, 2d session, serial 11747, September 20, 1954, vii.

80. William A. Brophy and Sophie D. Aberle, comp., *The Indian: America's Unfinished Business. Report of the Commission on the Rights, Liberties, and Responsibilities of the American Indian* (Norman: University of Oklahoma Press, 1966), 22, 180, 188; *The Voice of the American Indian: Declaration of Indian Purpose*, The American Indian Chicago Conference, June 13-20, 1961, 31.

81. *State Legal Jurisdiction in Indian Country*, Hearings before the Subcommittee on Indian Affairs of the Interior and Insular Affairs Committee, House, 82d Congress, 2d session, Feb. 28-29, 1952, 7-8, 25-26, 39, 42.

82. CSKT Minutes, Feb. 28, 1952, Box 7, 1944-1960.

83. CSKT Minutes, March 20, 1952 and Sept. 11, 1953, 1.

84. Indian Law and Order Conference, Aug. 31, 1953, in K. W. Bergan, coordinator, State of Montana, Department of Indian Affairs, *Annual Report*, December 31, 1954, unpaged.

85. Carole Goldberg, *Public Law 280: State Jurisdiction over Reservation Indians*. An American Indian Treaties Publication (Los Angeles: University of California, American Indian Culture and Research Center, 1975), 1-6; Fixico, *Termination and Relocation*, 111-112.

86. *Termination of Federal Supervision over Certain Tribes of Indians*, Joint Hearings before the Subcommittees of the Committees on Interior and Insular Affairs, 83rd Congress, 2d session, 1954. See all 12 Parts.

87. Record of 83rd Congress on Indian Affairs, Folder 1, Box 11, Wesley A. D'Ewart Papers, Collection 294, Merrill G. Burlingame Special Collections, Montana State University Libraries, Bozeman.

88. Francis Paul Prucha, *The Great Father: The United States Government and the American Indians*. Abridged edition (Lincoln: University of Nebraska Press, 1986), 348.

Chapter 2

1. Paul Charlo, Aneas Conco, and Sam Finley, members of Salish and Kootenai Tribes, to Senator James Murray, Oct. 13, 1943, Folder 7, Box 275, Murray Papers.

2. Assistant Commissioner of Indian Affairs William Zimmerman to Senator James Murray, Nov. 22, 1943, Folder 7, Box 275, Murray Papers.

3. Lorena M. Burgess, Paradise, Mont., to Senator Murray, Jan. 12, 1943, Folder 10, Box 1, Burgess Papers.

4. Isadore Matt, Gus White, et al, Ronan, Mont., to E. H. Moore, Committee on Indian Affairs, April 24, 1944, *Remove Restrictions on Indian Property*, Hearings before the Subcommittee of the Committee on Indian Affairs, Senate, 78th Congress, 2d session, January 10 and June 8, 1944, 147-148.

5. *Investigate Indian Affairs*, Hearings before the Committee on Indian Affairs, House, 78th Congress, 1st and 2d Sessions, 1943-1944, part 3, 451-457.

6. Ibid., part 3, 449-451; part 4, 295.

7. Thomas W. Cowger, *The National Congress of American Indians: The Founding Years* (Lincoln: University of Nebraska Press, 1999), 44.

8. The Montana Inter-Tribal Policy Board Meeting, Helena, April 17, 1953, in K. W. Bergan, coordinator, State of Montana, Department of Indian Affairs, *Annual Report*, December 31, 1954, unpaged.

9. "McDonald Elected Head of Northwest Indians," *Daily Missoulian* (Missoula, Montana), Oct. 23, 1960, 1,13.

10. S. 1682, 80th Congress, 1st session, Senate, July 21, 1947, Folder 27, Box 4, Burgess Papers.

11. James E. Hanson, "Flathead Group in Capitol for Hearings," *Daily Missoulian*, Feb. 21, 1954, 1, 22.

12. Mike Durglo, Sr., interview with author, Salish Longhouse, June 11, 1999. At the time of the interview, Durglo's son was a tribal council member. Doug Allard interview with author, Flathead Trading Post and Museum, St. Ignatius, May 22, 1999. Allard was a trader and the owner of the trading post and museum. Born in 1931, the college-educated Allard was the tribal secretary in the late 1970s. He chaired the tribe's Constitutional Convention Committee and the Pow Wow Committee.

13. D'Arcy McNickle to Lorena Burgess, Oct. 21, 1947, Folder 2, Box 8, Burgess Papers.

14. Revolving Credit Loans, CF 473, Eneas Granjo, Records of Flathead Agency, Box 601, Record Group 75, National Archives Rocky Mountain Regional Center, Denver. Granjo passed away at 74 in 1957, "Eneas Granjo, Tribal Official, Dies," *Daily Missoulian*, July 6, 1957, 1.

15. Minutes of the Meeting of the Tribal Council of the Confederated Salish and Kootenai Tribes of the Flathead Reservation, Sept. 16, 1946, quoted in Kenneth R. Philp, *Termination Revisited: American Indians on the Trail to Self-Determination, 1933-1953* (Lincoln: University of Nebraska Press, 1999), 69-70.

16. CSKT Minutes, Oct. 15, 1947, 3-5, Box 7, 1944-1960.

17. Office of Indian Affairs Circular Letter to All Superintendents, Aug. 21, 1945, 1-2, Folder FRC 14160, Box 484, Record Group 75, National Archives, Denver.

18. CSKT Minutes, June 5, 1947, 3.

19. Dorothy R. Parker, *Singing an Indian Song: A Biography of D'Arcy McNickle* (Lincoln: University of Nebraska Press, 1992), 9-27, 125.

20. Dorothy R. Parker, "D'Arcy McNickle: An Annotated Bibliography of His Published Articles and Book Reviews in a Biographical Context," John Lloyd Purdy, ed., *The Legacy of D'Arcy McNickle: Writer, Historian, Activist* (Norman: University of Oklahoma Press, 1996), 14, 18-19.

21. D'Arcy McNickle, "U.S. Indian Affairs — 1953," *America Indigena,* 13 (No. 4, 1953): 265-273.

22. D'Arcy McNickle, "The Indian in American Society," *Social Welfare Forum,* (1955): 177-179.

23. D'Arcy McNickle, "It's Almost Never Too Late," *Christian Century,* 74 (No. 8, Feb. 20, 1957): 227-228.

24. Thomas Main, Vice Chairman, Fort Belknap Tribal Council, Regional Secretary, Congress of American Indians, Member of the National Executive Council, Congress of American Indians, Hays, Mont., to Lorena Burgess, Paradise, Mont., Nov. 28, 1950, Folder 21, Box 2, Burgess Papers. Capital letters in the original.

25. Delegation Report, Meeting at Washington, D.C., CSKT Minutes, March 26-27, 1950.

26. Proceedings of the First Montana Indian Affairs Conference, Helena, June 22-23, 1951, Folder 6, Box 262, Murray Papers.

27. Revolving Credit Loans, CF 489, Walter W. McDonald, Box 602, Record Group 75, National Archives, Denver.

28. Noel Pichette interview with author, Salish Longhouse, St. Ignatius, Montana, June 11, 1999, Thurman Trosper interview with author, Trosper's home, Ronan, Montana, June 13, 1999.

29. Ronald L. Trosper, "Native American Boundary Maintenance: The Flathead Indian Reservation, Montana, 1860-1970," *Ethnicity,* 3 (No. 3, 1976): 257-259, 268; Theresa DeLeane O'Nell, *Disciplined Hearts: History, Identity, and Depression in an American Indian Community* (Berkeley: University of California Press, 1996), 51-52. Ronald Trosper is Thurman Trosper's son.

30. *Char-Koosta* (Dixon, Montana), Vol. 3 (No. 11, Sept. 1959): 1-4; Constitution and Bylaws of the Confederated Salish and Kootenai Tribes of the Flathead Reservation, Article II, Box 66, Record Group 75, National Archives, Denver.

31. Henry Matt, a member of tribal council, to Secretary of the Interior, Feb. 7, 1949, Folder 1, Box 276, Murray Papers.

32. James P. Nugent and Margery H. Brown, "Confederated Salish and Kootenai Tribes of the Flathead Reservation in Montana: An Analysis of Tribal Government in Relation to Pre-Reservation and Reservation Life of the Principal Tribes of Western Montana" (Seminar Paper, Indian Law Seminar, School of Law, University of Montana, 1975), 26.

33. *Congressional Record*, House, 82d Congress, 2d session, March 18, 1952, 2485 and July 1, 1952, 8788; *Congressional Record*, House, 83rd Congress, 1st session, July 10, 1953, A4246-47, where Bow quotes *Senate Report 310* of 1943 as a guideline for policy.

34. *House Report No. 2680: With Respect to the House Resolution Authorizing the Committee on Interior and Insular Affairs to Conduct an Investigation of the Bureau of Indian Affairs*, 83rd Congress, 2d session, September 20, 1954, serial 11747, 1-2, 5-6, 9-10.

35. Ibid., 3, 47-48, 321-22.

36. *FH Termination Hearings*, 777.

37. CSKT Minutes, Aug. 16, 1952, 5-6.

38. Minutes of Meeting of Assembly of Salish and Kootenai Tribes of the Flathead Reservation, May 6, 1948, St. Ignatius, Mont., cited in Ann Botch, "Mid-Century Flathead Termination Attempt: Senator James E. Murray's Reaction and Counterattack" (Seminar Paper, Department of History, University of Montana, 1973), 12

39. CSKT Minutes, Feb. 10, 1954.

40. Noel Pichette interview; John Peter Paul, interview with author, Salish Longhouse, June 11, 1999; Mary "Dolly" Linsebigler interview with author, Salish Longhouse, June 11, 1999. Mr. Paul was a walking dictionary of the Salish language.

41. *FH Termination Hearings*, 777-781.

42. *FH Termination Hearings*, 781-83, 833-4.

43. Mary "Dolly" Linsebigler interview.

44. *House Report 2680*, 322.

45. John Peter Paul interview.

46. CSKT Minutes, Jan. 5, 1952.

47. CSKT Minutes, Aug. 16, 1952, 1, 5.

48. CSKT Minutes, Aug. 16, 1952, 1-5.

49. CSKT Minutes, Aug. 16, 1952, 3-5.

50. CSKT Minutes, Nov. 14, 1953, 6.

51. CSKT Minutes, Sept. 4, 1952.

52. CSKT Minutes, Aug. 8, 1952, 1-2.

53. CSKT Minutes, Aug. 14, 1953.

54. CSKT Minutes, Sept. 18, 1952 and Jan. 8, 1953; also see *Char-Koosta*, 1 (No. 4, Feb. 1957): 1. Chairman McDonald claimed that the publication of *Char-Koosta* was prompted by termination to better let members know what was going on, *Char-Koosta*, 1 (No. 1, Nov. 1956): 1.

55. Area Director Paul Fickinger to Commissioner of Indian Affairs, Feb. 5, 1953, Folder Series 57, Box 465, Record Group 75, National Archives, Denver.

56. CSKT Minutes, Dec. 18, 1952.

57. "Indian Service Director Says Indians Use Double Talk At Meet Held in Billings," *The Flathead Courier* (Polson, Montana), Dec. 11, 1952, 1.

58. CSKT Minutes, Sept. 11, 1953, 3.

59. CSKT Minutes, Oct. 7, 1953, 5-7.

60. CSKT Minutes, Jan. 18, 1954, 3.

61. CSKT Minutes, Nov. 14, 1953, 1.

62. CSKT Minutes, Oct. 30, 1953.

63. CSKT Minutes, Nov. 14, 1953, 4.

64. CSKT Minutes, Nov. 14, 1953, 6.

65. CSKT Minutes, Nov. 14, 1953, 5.

66. CSKT Minutes, Jan. 18, 1954, 1-4.

67. Mike Durglo, Sr., and Mary "Dolly" Linsebigler interviews.

68. See Noel Pichette interview.

69. Botch, "Mid-Century Flathead Termination," 10.

70. Confederated Salish and Kootenai Tribes of the Flathead Reservation v. United States, Docket No. 61, 17 Indian Claims Commission 703, *Decisions of the Indian Claims Commission: Findings, Opinions, Orders and Final Awards of the United States Indian Claims Commission, 1948, et seq.* Abstracted by Frances L. Horn. Microform (New York: Clearwater Publication Company, 1973).

71. *Termination Hearings*, Part 6, Menominee Indians, 636. Watkins raised the issue on Flathead hearings as well, *FH Termination Hearings*, 827.

72. Ronald L. Trosper, "The Economic Impact of the Allotment Policy on the Flathead Indian Reservation," unpublished PhD dissertation, Harvard University, 1974, 212; Docket No. 61, Indian Claims Commission.

73. Cowger, *National Congress of American Indians*, 97.

74. CSKT Minutes, Jan. 27, 1954, 1-4.

75. CSKT Minutes, Jan. 26, 1954, 3.

76. *FH Termination Hearings*, 924.

77. Noel Pichette interview; also Mary "Dolly" Linsebigler and Doug Allard interviews.

78. Louis J. Tellier, Usk, Wash., Louis Curley, Spokane, Wash., and Robert Raymond, Spokane, Wash., to Mike Mansfield, U.S. Senate and Commissioner of Indian Affairs, March 12, 1954, CSKT Minutes, Apr. 3, 1954, 3-5 and Mike Mansfield Papers, Series IX, Container 25, K. Ross Toole Archives, Mansfield Library, University of Montana, Missoula.

79. Judith Gay Burgess Petitclerc, Everett, Wash., to whom it may concern, Jan. 6, 1955, Folder 12, Box 3, Burgess Papers.

80. Melford Ben Hull, Grand Coulee, Wash., to Lorena Burgess, May 8, 1954, Folder 11, Box 3, Burgess Papers.

81. Stephen Herzberg, "The Menominee Indians: From Treaty to Termination," *Wisconsin Magazine of History,* 60 (No. 4, Summer 1977): 318 and fn. 150, 319.

82. Berry interview, Steven C. Schulte, "Removing the Yoke of Government: E.Y. Berry and the Origins of the Indian Termination Policy," *South Dakota History,* 14 (No. 1, Spring 1984): 56.

83. *Termination Hearings,* Part 1, Utah Indians, 17, 30.

84. *FH Termination Hearings,* 777.

85. Bergan, *Annual Report,* December 31, 1952, 37.

86. *FH Termination Hearings,* 906-915, quote 915.

87. *FH Termination Hearings,* 916-920, 939; See Constitution and By-laws, Article IV, Section 5, 2, National Archives, Denver.

88. *FH Termination Hearings,* 924-40.

89. *FH Termination Hearings,* 941-954, 958-962, 975, quote 945.

90. *FH Termination Hearings,* 947-950, 972-978.

91. Walter McDonald, Chairman, Walter Morigeau, Vice-Chairman, Jerome Hewankorn, Councilman, George Tunison, Attorney, "Re: H.R. 7319, Memo for Confederated Salish and Kootenai Tribes of the Flathead Reservation, Montana," Feb. 19, 1954, 1, 8, Folder 2, Box 276, Murray Papers; James E. Hanson, "Flathead Group in Capital for Hearings," *Daily Missoulian,* Feb. 21, 1954, 1, 22.

92. *FH Termination Hearings,* 978-988.

93. *FH Termination Hearings,* 946, 980-986.

94. *FH Termination Hearings,* 967-71. Hewankorn's name is misspelled Hewaukan in the hearings transcript, but there is no doubt this is the same person, Thompson Smith, historical consultant to Salish Culture Committee, conversation with author, Salish Longhouse, St. Ignatius, Montana, June 11, 1999.

95. Revolving Credit Loans, CF 504, Jerome Hewankorn, Box 602, Record Group 75, National Archives, Denver.

96. *FH Termination Hearings,* 1005-1015. Charrier had no Indian blood, Forrest Stone, Superintendent, to Senator James Murray, Apr. 2, 1953, Folder 1, Box 276, Murray Papers.

97. CSKT Minutes, Nov. 14, 1953, 14, and Nov. 25, 1953.

98. Vera Voorhies to Senator James Murray, Dec. 4, 1953, Folder 1, Box 276, Murray Papers; File 17095–310.4, box 9, Central Classifield Files, 1953-1954, Record Group 75, National Archives, Washington, D.C.

99. *FH Terminaton Hearings,* 821, 891-93, 931-32.

100. Herzberg, "Menominee Indians," 306-07, 320.

101. Senator James Murray to Chairman Walter McDonald, June 16, 1954, Folder 2, Box 276, Murray Papers.

102. Noel Pichette interview; on the majority opposing see Mike Durglo, Sr., interview; on prejudice see Mary "Dolly" Linsebigler interview.

Chapter 3

1. Guide to Wesley D'Ewart Papers, Wesley D'Ewart Papers, Collection 294, Merrill G. Burlingame Special Collections, Montana State University Libraries, Bozeman; "Red Web over Congress," Folder 16, Box 192, Murray Papers; *Nomination of Wesley A. D'Ewart to be Assistant Secretary of the Interior,* Hearings before the Committee on Interior and Insular Affairs, Senate, 84th Congress, 2d session, July 11, 13, 1956.

2. Luella Johnk, Billings, Mont., to Representative Wesley D'Ewart, Feb. 24 and Mar. 5, 1947, Reel 59, *The Indian Rights Association Papers* (Glen Rock, N.J.: Microfilming Corporation of America, 1975).

3. Carling Malouf, "Turn the Indians Loose?" 1, 4, Mimeograph, Montana State University, Missoula, 1954. In the 1950s, University of Montana was still called Montana State University.

4. *State Legal Jurisdiction in Indian Country,* Hearings before the Subcommittee on Indian Affairs of the Interior and Insular Affairs Committee, House, 82d Congress, 2d session, Feb. 28-29, 1952, 8.

5. "Tribal Hearing Gives Congress Many Ideas and Information on Removal of Supervision," *The Flathead Courier* (Polson, Montana), Oct. 22, 1953, 1.

6. Vera A. Dupuis Voorhies, Anna Weivoda, Lorena M. Burgess, et al, Polson, Montana, to William H. Harrison, Chairman, Subcommittee of the Interior and Insular Affairs, Nov. 30, 1953, Folder 8, Box 240, Metcalf Papers.

7. *FH Termination Hearings,* 886-8, 910-11, 938-40, 1005.

8. "D'Ewart Talks on National Problems at Informal Meet Held at The Ranch Saturday," *The Flathead Courier,* April 15, 1954, 1.

9. Donald Spritzer, *Senator James E. Murray and the Limits of Post-War Liberalism* (New York: Garland Publishing, 1985), 2-22.

10. Ann Botch, "Mid-Century Flathead Termination Attempt: Senator James E. Murray's Reaction and Counterattack" (Seminar Paper, Department of History, University of Montana, 1973), 9.

11. Meeting of the officials from public school districts enrolling Indian children, Billings, Feb. 12, 1949, Folder 3, Box 262, Murray Papers.

12. Senator James E. Murray to Board of County Commissioners, Big Horn County, Montana, Feb. 4, 1947, Folder 1, Box 262, Murray Papers.

13. Botch, "Mid-Century Flathead Termination," 4.

14. Senator James E. Murray to N. C. Briggs, Administrator, State Department of Public Welfare, Montana, Feb. 17, 1950, Folder 4, Box 262, Murray Papers.

15. Botch, "Mid-Century Flathead Termination," 34-35.

16. *Federal Indian Policy*, Hearings before the Subcommittee on Indian Affairs of the Committee on Interior and Insular Affairs, Senate, 85th Congress, 1st session, 1957, 47-63, 92-94.

17. *Congressional Record*, Senate, 86th Congress, 1st session, Senate, March 2, 1959, 3104-05, 3178.

18. *FH Termination Hearings*, 829.

19. Extension of Remarks of James E. Murray, *Congressional Record*, Senate, 83rd Congress, 2d session, April 20, 1954, A2940.

20. James E. Murray to Dennis Dellwo, Secretary, Flathead Irrigation District, Feb. 9, 1954, Folder 4, Box 351, Murray Papers.

21. *FH Termination Hearings*, 890-892.

22. *Congressional Record*, Senate, 86th Congress, 1st session, Senate, Sept. 10, 1959, 18889-90.

23. *Indian Land Transactions: An Analysis of the Problems and Effects of Our Diminishing Indian Land Base, 1948-57*, Senate Committee on Interior and Insular Affairs Print, 85th Congress, 2d session, Dec. 1, 1958, xvii, 1.

24. Donald A. Ritchie, "The Senate of Mike Mansfield," *Montana: The Magazine of Western History,* 48 (No. 4, Winter 1998): 50-51, 55, 60-61.

25. Senator Mansfield comments on SCR 12, April 28, 1959, Folder 17, Container 28, Series VIII, Mike Mansfield Papers, K. Ross Toole Archives, Mansfield Library, University of Montana, Missoula.

26. *Congressional Record*, 84th Congress, 2d session, Senate, Jan. 12, 1956, 379-82; *Congressional Record*, 86th Congress, 2d session, Senate, Jan. 22, 1960, 1070.

27. Senator Mike Mansfield to Wesley A. D'Ewart, Assistant Secretary of the Interior, Jan. 6, 1955, *Congressional Record*, 84th Congress, 2d session, Senate, Jan. 12, 1956, 382.

28. *Congressional Record*, 86th Congress, 2d session, Senate, May 5, 1960, 9549.

29. "Introduction," Metcalf Papers. At the time Metcalf earned his degree, the university was still Montana State.

30. Lee Metcalf to Hildur Lang, Polson, Montana, May 31, 1955, 1-2, Folder 7, Box 240, Metcalf Papers.

31. Representative Lee Metcalf and his executive secretary Brit Englund go through Metcalf's bulky file on Flathead termination, non-dated transcript for a radio broadcast, (filed under 1954), Folder 1, Box 225, Metcalf Papers.

32. Lee Metcalf, "Termination in 83rd Congress," *Juvenile Delinquency (Indians)*, Hearings before the Subcommittee to Investigate Juvenile Delinquency of the Committee on the Judiciary Pursuant to SR 62, Senate, 84th Congress, 1st session, March 11, April 28-30, 1955, 419-21.

33. "Blackmail Charged to Indian Bureau," *New York Times*, Sept. 17, 1958, 75.

34. Lee Metcalf, "The Need for Revision of Federal Policy in Indian Affairs," *Indian Truth* (Indian Rights Association, Philadelphia), 35 (No. 1, Jan.-Mar. 1958): 1.

35. Statement of Lee Metcalf before the Subcommittee on Indian Affairs of the House Interior and Insular Affairs Committee, May 15, 1959, Folder 7, Box 605, Metcalf Papers.

36. Extension of Remarks of Lee Metcalf, *Congressional Record*, 84th Congress, 2d session, House, Jan. 16, 1956, 627.

37. NBC Kaleidoscope: "The American Stranger," by Robert McCormick, Nov. 16, 1958, 5-9, manuscript in Folder 4, Box 264, Murray Papers.

38. "Statement by the Department of Interior concerning the 'Kaleidoscope' TV Program of Nov. 16, 1958," 11, 22, Folder 4, Box 264, Murray Papers.

39. Spritzer, *Senator James Murray*, 234, 242; Larry J. Hasse, "Termination and Assimilation: Federal Indian Policy, 1943 to 1961" (Ph.D. dissertation, Washington State University, 1974), DAI 7416367, 63-64, 124.

40. Hasse, "Termination and Assimilation," 121-122, 236.

41. Spritzer, *Senator James Murray*, 155.

42. *Interior Department Appropriation Bill for 1950*, Hearings before a Subcommittee of the Committee on Appropriations, Senate, 81st Congress, 1st session, Part 2, 1950, 1607-36.

43. Confederated Salish and Kootenai Tribes of the Flathead Reservation, *Background of the Problem of the Indians of the Flathead Reservation and Their Dam Sites* (Dixon, Mont.: Confederated Salish and Kootenai Tribes, 1960), 1-11.

44. Confederated Salish and Kootenai Tribes of the Flathead Reservation, *As Long As the Waters Flow . . . : Kerr Dam, Power on the Flathead, a Study of Flathead Hydroelectric Development* (Dixon, Mont.: Confederated Salish and Kootenai Tribes, 1962), 4-6.

45. *Char-Koosta* (Dixon, Montana), 1 (No. 4, Feb. 1957): 2-3; 4 (No. 1, Dec. 1959): 2; 4 (No. 2, Feb. 1960): 1; CSKT Minutes, Oct. 4, 1957, 1-2, Box 7, 1944-1960,

46. "Opposition to the Paradise Dam, Writings by Lorena Burgess," Folder 8, Box 4, Burgess Papers.

47. Mary M. Condon, Superintendent of Public Instruction, Helena, on S. 2750 and H.R. 7319, 1-3, filed under 1954, Folder 1, Box 225, Metcalf Papers; *FH Termination Hearings*, 895-896.

48. W. J. Fouse, Administrator, Department of Public Welfare, Helena, FH Termination Hearings, 897; Fouse to Lee Metcalf, US Representative from Montana, May 26, 1954, Folder 8, Box 240, Metcalf Papers.

49. W. J. Fouse, Administrator, Department of Public Welfare to Governor Aronson, Dec. 29, 1953, K. W. Bergan, coordinator, State of Montana, Department of Indian Affairs, *Annual Report*, December 31, 1954, unpaged.

50. John C. Harrison, President, Montana Tuberculosis Association, Helena, Feb. 20, 1954, to Chairman of the Joint Congressional Committees, *FH Termination Hearings*, 901.

51. K. W. Bergan, Coordinator of Indian Affairs, State of Montana, Helena, to Lee Metcalf, U.S. Congressman, Feb. 18, 1954, 1-2, Folder 8, Box 240, Metcalf Papers; *FH Termination Hearings*, 897.

52. K. W. Bergan, State Coordinator of Indian Affairs to Governor Hugo Aronson, Dec. 31, 1953, Bergan, *Annual Report*, December 31, 1954, unpaged.

53. K. W. Bergan to members of Inter-Tribal Policy Board, not dated, in ibid.; also Malouf, "Turn the Indians Loose?" 1.

54. Address of Governor John W. Bonner before the Governors Conference on Indian Affairs at Houston, Texas, July 2, 1952, 3-5, Folder 19, Box 2, Burgess Papers.

55. J. Hugo Aronson, Governor, Telegram to Lee Metcalf, Feb. 23, 1954, Folder 8, Box 240, Metcalf Papers; *FH Termination Hearings*, 898.

56. Oliver R. Brown, Chairman, Board of Lake County Commissioners, Polson, Al Libra, Sanders County Attorney, Thompson Falls, and Jean A. Turnage, Lake County Attorney, *FH Termination Hearings*, 899-900.

57. Board of County Commissioners, Lake County, Montana to Senator James Murray, Dec. 8, 1947, Folder 8, Box 275, Murray Papers.

58. J. A. Turnage, Lake County Attorney, to Senator Murray, March 15, 1954, Folder 3, Box 263, Murray Papers.

59. Ethel T. Terry, Chairman, Legislation Committee, Lake County Democratic Committee, Polson, to Lee Metcalf, Apr. 16, 1955, Folder 7, Box 240, Metcalf Papers.

60. William C. Newton, Area Social Worker, to John W. Cragun, c/o Wilkinson, Cragun, Barker and Hawkins, Washington, D.C., July 3, 1956, 7, Folder 2, Box 241, Metcalf Papers.

61. Dennis A. Dellwo, Secretary, Flathead Irrigation District, to Mike Mansfield, Feb. 3, 1954, *FH Termination Hearings*, 904-5.

62. Raymond Gray, Belt, Mont., to Senator James Murray, Feb. 26, 1954, Folder 2, Box 276, Murray Papers.

63. Emma Koliha, Great Falls, Letter to the Editor, *Great Falls Tribune* (Great Falls, Montana), July 5, 1954, 6.

64. Dorothy Bohn, Chairman of Indian Affairs Committee, Cascade County Community Council, to Senator Murray, June 28, 1954, Folder 6, Box 351, Murray Papers.

65. Dorothy Bohn, "'Liberating' the Indian: Euphemism for a Land Grab," *Nation*, 178 (No. 8, Feb. 20, 1954): 150-151.

66. Dorothy Bohn to Lee Metcalf, Sept. 30, 1955, 1-3, Folder 6, Box 605, Metcalf Papers.

67. James J. Flaherty, Chairman, The Montana Committee Against Termination, "Obligation of Federal Trust," *Social Order,* 5 (Feb. 1955): 10-12.

68. Statement of Richard Shipman, Vice President, Montana Farmer's Union, *FH Termination Hearings,* 785-794, 799-831.

69. Roy R. Taber, Ronan, Montana, to Senator Murray, Jan. 8, 1954, Folder 2, Box 276, Murray Papers.

70. John Cragun, Wilkinson, Cragun, Barker & Hawkins, to Montana Congressional Delegation, Jan. 15, 1957, Folder 7, Box 263, Murray Papers and Folder 4, Box 230, Metcalf Papers; James Murray to Commissioner Glenn Emmons, Aug. 15, 1958, Folder 3, Box 264, Murray Papers.

71. "Indian Freedom A National Question," editorial by "H. M.," *The Flathead Courier,* Jan. 14, 1954, 2; "52 Years — $1 Billion Later," editorial by "H. M.," *The Flathead Courier,* Feb. 11, 1954, 2.

72. "An Indian Proposal," editorial by "H. M.," *The Flathead Courier,* Mar. 4, 1954, 2; "The Indian Workshops," editorial by "H. M.," *The Flathead Courier,* May 6, 1954, 2.

73. "Indians Aren't 'Old People'," *The Ronan Pioneer,* March 11, 1954, 2. Published weekly in Ronan, Montana, by Ray M. Loman, editor.

74. Avis Anderson, "The Effect of the Termination Policy of the 1950's on the Landless Indians of Montana," Seminar Paper in American History, University of Montana, no date, 2-4.

75. *FH Terminaton Hearings,* 880-882; Commissioner Glenn Emmons to Montana Congressional Delegation, Apr. 18, 1957, Folder 1, Box 286, Murray Papers; Statement by the Department of the Interior concerning the "Kaleidoscope" TV Program of Nov. 16, 1958, Folder 4, Box 264, Murray Papers.; Secretary of the Interior Douglas McKay to Senator Mansfield, Feb. 8, 1956, Container 47, Series X, Mike Mansfield Papers.

76. Max Gubatayao, Chairman, Friends of Hill 57, Great Falls, to Senator Mansfield, May 7, 1958, Container 47, Series X, Mike Mansfield Papers; Gubatayao to Walter McDonald, Chairman, Flathead Tribal Council, Nov. 27, 1957, Folder 7, Box 240, Metcalf Papers.

77. Senators Murray and Mansfield to Commissioner Emmons, Apr. 25, 1957, Folder 1, Box 286, Murray Papers; Dorothy R. Parker, *Singing an Indian Song: A Biography of D'Arcy McNickle* (Lincoln: University of Nebraska Press, 1992), 71.

78. Joan Bishop, "From Hill 57 to Capitol Hill: 'Making the Sparks Fly': Sister Providencia Tolan's Drive on Behalf of Montana's Off-Reservation Indians, 1950-1970," *Montana: The Magazine of Western History,* 43 (No. 3, Summer 1993): 23; Malouf, "Turn the Indians Loose?" 4.

79. Bergan, *Annual Report,* Dec. 31, 1952, 3-25; Address of Governor John W. Bonner, 1952, 6-7, Folder 19, Box 2, Burgess Papers.

80. Montana Inter-Tribal Policy Board Meeting, Helena, Feb. 7, 1954; and Montana Report on Termination Read by Inter-Tribal Policy Board

Representative, Salish-Kootenai Tribal Member, Steve DeMers, Governor's Conference on Interstate Indian Council, Sun Valley, Idaho, Sept. 30 — Oct. 2, 1954, in Bergan, *Annual Report*, December 31, 1954, unpaged.

81. Statement of Freda Beazley, Secretary, Montana Inter-Tribal Policy Board, *FH Termination Hearings*, 995-996.

82. Frederick E. Hoxie, *Parading Through History: The Making of the Crow Nation in America, 1805-1935* (Cambridge: Cambridge University Press, 1995), 253-261, 326-339.

83. Robert Yellowtail, "Open Letter to All Montana Indians," no date, and D'Ewart's comments to former, Folder 3, Box 2, Wesley D'Ewart Papers.

84. The Montana Inter-Tribal Policy Board Meeting, Apr. 17, 1953, Helena, in Bergan, *Annual Report*, December 31, 1954, unpaged.

85. Proceedings of the Governor's Advisory Council Meetings on Indian Affairs, Helena, Oct. 16-17, 1951, Folder 6, Box 262, Murray Papers; *Report of Proceedings: Dillon S. Myer of Ohio to Be Commissioner of Indian Affairs*, Hearing held before Committee on Interior and Insular Affairs, Senate, 81st Congress, 2d session, April 10, 1950, 73, 79.

86. Robert Yellowtail, Chairman, Crow Tribal Council, "Questions Decided by the Lone Wolf Decision (187 U.S. 553)," no date, Folder 23, Box 4, Burgess Papers.

87. Statement of David Higgins, Member, Blackfeet Reservation and Member, Montana House of Representatives, *FH Termination Hearings*, 995-1004.

88. Kenneth R. Philp, *Termination Revisited: American Indians on the Trail to Self-Determination, 1933-1953* (Lincoln: University of Nebraska Press, 1999), 125-139.

89. Allen Foreman, Chairman of the Klamath Tribes, et al, "Termination: An Account of the Termination of the Klamath Reservation from the Tribes' Point of View," *The Herald and News* (Klamath Falls, Oregon), Nov. 1, 1999, 1-6.

90. Philp, *Termination Revisited*, 158.

91. Hasse, "Termination and Assimilation," 218, 222.

92. Theodore Stern, *The Klamath Tribe: A People and Their Reservation* (Seattle: University of Washington Press, 1965), 249; Lawrence E. Davies, "Oregon Indians Split on Future: Klamath Tribe Views Chance for Full Citizenship with Eagerness and Dismay," *New York Times*, June 19, 1955, 76; Donald L. Fixico, *Termination and Relocation: Federal Indian Policy, 1945 to 1960* (Albuquerque: University of New Mexico Press, 1986), 117, 125.

93. Foreman, "Termination," 2-3; Donald L. Fixico, *The Invasion of Indian Country in the Twentieth Century: American Capitalism and Tribal Natural Resources* (Niwot: University Press of Colorado, 1998), 81-85; Senator Wayne Morse's view in *Congressional Record*, 80th Congress, 1st session, Senate, May 2, 1947, 4458; Hasse, "Termination and Assimilation," 220.

94. Mrs. Wade Crawford, "An Indian Talks Back," *American Forests,* 63 (No. 7, July 1957): 48-49 (quote); *Emancipation of Indians,* Hearings before the Subcommittee on Indian Affairs of the Committee on Public Lands, House, 80th Congress, 1st session, April 18-21 and May 15, 1947, 87.

95. Foreman, "Termination," 2-3; Fixico, *Invasion of Indian Country,* 81-85; Verne Ray, "The Klamath Oppose Liquidation," *American Indian,* 4 (No. 4, 1948): 22; *Emancipation of Indians,* 82.

96. Davies, "Oregon Indians Split," 76; "Klamath Indians Act on Freedom: Referendum Picks Committee to Deal with Management on End of U.S. Controls," *New York Times,* July 10, 1955, 64; Harold Fey and D'Arcy McNickle, *Indians and Other Americans: Two Ways of Life Meet.* Revised edition (New York: Harper and Row, 1970), 175.

97. Seldon E. Kirk, Official Chairman, General Council, and Jesse Lee Kirk, Official Chairman, Klamath Tribal Business Committee, to the Superintendent, Klamath Reservation, Feb. 20, 1947, 1-2, Folder 21, Box 4, Burgess Papers.

98. Forrest Cooper, "Rough Draft of Bill Proposed for Liquidation of the Klamath Indian Reservation, Klamath County, Lake County, Oregon," Folder 21, Box 4, Burgess Papers.

99. Philp, *Termination Revisited,* 146; Hasse, "Termination and Assimilation," 221.

100. *Termination Hearings,* Part 4, Klamath, 260, 275, 294, 303.

101. Fixico, *Invasion of Indian Country,* 85.

102. "Klamath Indians Act on Freedom," *New York Times,* July 10, 1955, 64.

103. Lawrence E. Davies, "Indians in Oregon Give U.S. a Riddle: Committees Seek Solution as Freedom Nears for Tribe on Klamath Lands," *New York Times,* Feb. 10, 1957, 46; Hasse, "Termination and Assimilation," 226.

104. Fixico, Invasion of Indian Country, 91, 96; Richard Neuberger, "How Oregon Rescued a Forest," *Harper's Magazine,* 218 (No. 1307, April 1959), 49; *Federal Indian Policy,* 267.

105. Stanford Research Institute, *Preliminary Planning for Termination of Federal Control Over the Klamath Indian Tribe,* SRI Project No. I-1440 (Menlo Park, Calif., 1956), 3-4.

106. Fixico, *Invasion of Indian Country,* 88; Ray, "Klamath Oppose," 15-19.

107. Stanford Research Institute, *Preliminary Planning,* 10; Foreman, "Termination," 4-6; William Thomas Trulove, "Economics of Paternalism: Federal Policy and the Klamath Indians" (Ph.D. dissertation, University of Oregon, 1973), DAI 7412965, 200

108. Foreman, "Termination," 7-8; Charles Crane Brown, "Identification of Selected Problems of Indians Residing in Klamath County, Oregon: An Examination of Data Generated since Termination of the Klamath Reservation"

(Ph.D. dissertation, University of Oregon, 1973), DAI 7412926, abstract; on the changes in society, Fixico, *Invasion of Indian Country*, 97.

109. Nicholas Peroff, *Menominee DRUMS: Tribal Termination and Restoration, 1954-1974* (Norman: University of Oklahoma Press, 1982), 80-83.

110. George and Louise Spindler, *Dreamers Without Power: The Menomini Indians*, Case Studies in Cultural Anthropology (New York: Holt, Rinehart and Winston, 1971), 202-204; Deborah Shames, ed., *Freedom with Reservation: The Menominee Struggle to Save Their Land and People* (Madison: Wisconsin Indian Legal Services, 1972), 5-11; on religious motives, Alvin Josephy, Jr., conversation with author, Western History Association Conference, Albuquerque, October 1994.

111. Robert Edgerton, "Menominee Termination: Observations on the End of a Tribe," *Human Organization*, 21 (No. 1, Spring 1962): 11-12; Peroff, *Menominee DRUMS*, 33, 98.

112. Edgerton, "Menominee Termination," 13-14; David W. Ames and Burton R. Fisher, "The Menominee Termination Crisis: Barriers in the Way of a Rapid Cultural Transition," *Human Organization*, 18 (No. 3, Fall 1959): 107; Peroff, *Menominee DRUMS*, 97-98.

113. Peroff, *Menominee DRUMS*, 100-102.

114. Ibid., 53-55, 105; *Congressional Record*, 83rd Congress, 1st session, Senate, July 24, 1953, 9743; Stephen Herzberg, "The Menominee Indians: From Treaty to Termination," *Wisconsin Magazine of History*, 60 (No. 4, Summer 1977), 313.

115. *Termination Hearings*, Part 6, Menominee, 651-658; Peroff, *Menominee DRUMS*, 89-93; Herzberg, "Menominee Indians," 322-329.

116. Rep. Henry R. Reuss before House Subcommittee on Indian Affairs, Feb. 27, 1956, Reel 45, frames 132-135, *The John Collier Papers*, Microfilm edition (Sanford, N.C.: Microfilming Corporation of America, 1980).

117. *Congressional Record*, 83rd Congress, 1st session, House, Aug. 1, 1953, 10931; *Termination Hearings*, Part 6, Menominee, 605.

118. *Termination Hearings*, Part 6, Menominee, 594-596; *Congressional Record*, 85th Congress, 2d session, House, June 24, 1958, 12080, and 86th Congress, 2nd session, Senate, March 23, 1960, 6332, Senate, Aug. 25, 1960, 17601. Laird represented Wisconsin's seventh district, which included Shawano County where the Menominee Reservation was situated.

119. Herzberg, "Menominee Indians," 318; Fixico, *Termination and Relocation*, 98-99, 114.

120. Peroff, *Menominee DRUMS*, 8, 113-117, 129-133, 175.

121. Parker M. Nielson, *The Dispossessed: Cultural Genocide of the Mixed-Blood Utes: An Advocate's Chronicle* (Norman: University of Oklahoma Press, 1998), 42-43; Carolyn Grattan-Aiello, "Senator Arthur V. Watkins and the Termination of Utah's Southern Paiute Indians," *Utah Historical Quarterly*, 63 (No. 3, Summer 1995): 269-275.

122. Grattan-Aiello, "Senator Arthur Watkins," 273.

123. Nielson, *Dispossessed*, 43, 137; R. Warren Metcalf, "Arthur V. Watkins and the Indians of Utah: A Study of Federal Termination Policy" (Ph.D. dissertation, Arizona State University, 1995), DAI 9511697, 5, 115.

124. Nielson, *Dispossessed*, ix, 70; Metcalf, "Arthur Watkins," iv, 172, 179-186, 226-228.

125. Nielson, *Dispossessed*, 43-48, 83-90, 100, 115, 125.

Chapter 4

1. Joane Nagel, *American Indian Ethnic Renewal: Red Power and the Resurgence of Identity and Culture* (New York: Oxford University Press, 1996), 12, 115-125, 199, 220; also see James J. Rawls, *Chief Red Fox Is Dead: A History of Native Americans Since 1945* (Fort Worth: Harcourt Brace College Publishers, 1996), 53-56.

2. George Pierre Castile, *To Show Heart: Native American Self-Determination and Federal Indian Policy, 1960-1975* (Tucson: University of Arizona Press, 1998), xi-xix, 25, 32, 48, 81, 92, 178; Rawls, *Chief Red Fox*, 57-60.

3. Noel Pichette interview with author, Salish Longhouse, St. Ignatius, June 11, 1999.

4. James J. Lopach, Margery Hunter Brown, and Richmond L. Clow, *Tribal Government Today: Politics on Montana Indian Reservations*. Revised edition (Niwot: University Press of Colorado, 1998), Table 11.1, 204; Patti Sessions, assistant editor of Char-Koosta, on www.montana.com/people/home2/sti4623/www/ps4.html.

5. Theresa DeLeane O'Nell, *Disciplined Hearts: History, Identity, and Depression in an American Indian Community* (Berkeley: University of California Press, 1996), 45-55, footnote 1, 221.

6. CSKT Minutes, Oct. 4, 1957, 1-3, Box 7, 1944-1960.

7. Denn Curran, "Flathead: 'This Is Probably the Least Typical Indian Reservation in the United States'," *Missoulian*, Apr. 20, 1969, 28.

8. CSKT Minutes, Oct. 4, 1957, 3.

9. Steven C. DeMers, "Keynote Address before the Northwest Affiliated Tribe Convention," Oct. 19-22, 1960, Missoula, in Governors' Interstate Indian Council, "Study on Termination of Federal Supervision on Indian Reservations," Report Submitted by Committee at Missoula, Montana Conference, Aug. 13-16, 1961, 7-8, at the Confederated Salish Kootenai Tribes Collection, McNickle Library, Salish Kootenai College, Pablo.

10. John W. Reynolds, Attorney General, the State of Wisconsin, to K. W. Bergan, Coordinator, Indian Affairs, State of Montana, Sept. 14, 1960, in GIIC, "Study on Termination," 16-18.

11. GIIC, "Study on Termination," 29-30.

12. "Governors' Interstate Indian Council, Resolution No. 1, Palm Springs, CA, Nov. 13-16, 1960," *Annual Report of the Arizona Commission of Indian Affairs*, 1961, 28.

13. Mary "Dolly" Linsebigler interview.

14. Noel Pichette interview; John Peter Paul, and Mike Durglo, Sr., interviews with author, Salish Longhouse, St. Ignatius, June 11, 1999.

15. Lopach, Brown, Clow, *Tribal Government Today*, 254.

16. Thurman Trosper interview. Born in 1917, Trosper joined Marine Corps in World War II and worked for the United States Forest Service for 22 years. After retirement, he moved back to the reservation and was active in many fields and organizations.

17. Lopach, Brown, Clow, *Tribal Government Today*, 253-254.

18. James B. Horner, Ronan, Mont., to Lee Metcalf of Montana, U.S. Senate, May 2, 1972, Folder 1, Box 220, Metcalf Papers.

19. Jaye Johnson, Ronan, Mont., to Lee Metcalf, United States Senate, Feb. 15, 1972, Folder 1, Box 220, Metcalf Papers.

20. Vi Walchuk, Ronan, Mont., to Lee Metcalf, Apr. 21, 1972, Folder 1, Box 220, Metcalf Papers.

21. Donald and Carrie Jensen, Elmo, Mont., to Senator Lee Metcalf, Apr. 20, 1972, Folder 1, Box 220, Metcalf Papers.

22. John D. Crow, Deputy Commissioner, Bureau of Indian Affairs, to Lee Metcalf, United States Senate, July 17, 1972; Crow to Metcalf, June 9, 1972; Crow to Metcalf, June 5, 1972; all in Folder 1, Box 220, Metcalf Papers.

23. Norene Mosley, Mayor, City of Polson, to Forrest Anderson, Governor, State of Montana, Apr. 14, 1972; Gerald L. Newgard, Polson Chamber of Commerce, to Lee Metcalf, U.S. Senate, Apr. 14, 1972; both in Folder 1, Box 220, Metcalf Papers.

24. Albert J. Cramer, Polson, Mont., to Lee Metcalf, United States Senate, Apr. 22, 1972, Folder 1, Box 220, Metcalf Papers.

25. Quoted in Curran, "Flathead," 27.

26. Robert M. Peregoy, "Jurisdictional Aspects of Indian Reserved Water Rights in Montana and on the Flathead Reservation after Adsit," *American Indian Culture and Research Journal*, 7 (No. 1, 1983): 49, 58-62; Lopach, Brown, Clow, *Tribal Government Today*, 180-181.

27. Peregoy, "Jurisdictional Aspects," 71-77; Lopach, Brown, Clow, *Tribal Government Today*, 251.

28. Lopach, Brown, Clow, *Tribal Government Today*, 180; O'Nell, *Disciplined Hearts*, 22-23; Donald L. Parman, *Indians and the American West in the Twentieth Century* (Bloomington: Indiana University Press, 1994), 178-180 (quote); Rawls, *Chief Red Fox*, 160.

29. Covey quoted in Parman, *Indians and American West*, 181; also see Rawls, *Chief Red Fox*, 160.

30. Lucille Trosper Otter, Salish elder, quoted in Rawls, *Chief Red Fox*, 160. Otter was Thurman Trosper's sister.

31. "Neighbors Draft Position Paper on Tribal Sovereignty," Feb. 22, 1996, 1-4, given to author by "Neighbors" member Rob Sand, Charlo, Montana, June 12, 1999.

32. CSKT minutes, Dec. 18, 1970, 3.

33. E. W. Morigeau, *Valley Creek: The Autobiography of E. W. Morigeau. A True Story of a Flathead Reservation Indian* (Polson, Montana, Privately published by Walter Douglas Morigeau, 2002), 93-96.

34. "Liquidation Petition Format Approved at Ronan Wednesday," *Missoulian*, Jan. 22, 1971, 11; Marge Anderson, "Tribal Liquidation Includes 'Intangibles'," *Missoulian*, Jan. 16, 1971, 5.

35. Marge Anderson, "Tribal Attorney Admits Termination No Answer," *Missoulian*, Feb. 1, 1971, 7.

36. Marge Anderson, "Tribe May Liquidate Holdings In Flathead,"*Missoulian*, Jan. 15, 1971, 1, 2.

37. Joe McDonald, "Don't Terminate," Letters to the Editor, *Missoulian*, Jan. 20, 1971, 4. Joe McDonald was later the president of the Salish Kootenai College.

38. Marge Anderson, "Indians Oppose Liquidation," *Missoulian*, Jan. 23, 1971, 1, 2.

39. Marge Anderson, "Tribal Liquidation Advocates Speak Up," *Missoulian*, Jan. 20, 1971, 7.

40. "Liquidation Petition Format Approved at Ronan Wednesday," *Missoulian*, Jan. 22, 1971, 11.

41. Marge Anderson, "Tribal Assets Petitions Mailed to 1,000 Indians," *Missoulian*, Jan. 27, 1971, 7; "Dupuis Quitting Liquidation Group," *Missoulian*, Jan. 28, 1971, 1.

42. Marge Anderson, "Issues and Indians Stand," *Missoulian*, Jan. 31, 1971, 12; "Controversy Continues on Tribal Withdrawal Proposal," *The Flathead Courier*, Feb. 4, 1971, 2.

43. CSKT minutes, Feb. 5, 1971, 7 (first quote); Marge Anderson, "Morigeau Voted Off Indian Committees," *Missoulian*, Feb. 6, 1971, 7 (second quote).

44. "Off-Reservation Indians Are for Optional Withdrawal," *Ronan Pioneer*, Feb. 25, 1971, 1.

45. CSKT minutes, March 6, 1971, 1-6.

46. Gary Langley, "Problems Seen In Payment of $22 Million," *Missoulian*, May 10, 1972, 1.

47. CSKT minutes, April 2, 1971, 2-11.

48. Morigeau, *Valley Creek*, 109-113, 127.

49. Ibid., 127-131. Mickey Pablo (1951-2000) served as a council chairman for the better part of the period 1984-2000.

50. Thurman Trosper interview with the author, Ronan, Mont., June 13, 1999.

51. Al Hewankorn, Sadie Saloway, Francis Auld interviews with author, Kootenai Community Center, Elmo, Mont., June 23, 2004, and Adeline Mathias interview, Dayton, Mont., June 25, 2004.

52. Thurman Trosper interview.

53. John Peter Paul (first quote), Noel Pichette, Mary "Dolly" Linsebigler and Thurman Trosper (second quote) interviews.

54. Ruth Quequesah, "Locals Oppose Tribal Takeover of Bison Range," *Char-Koosta News*, 34 (No. 22, March 20, 2003), 1.

55. Jennifer Greene, "Tribes Prepare for Meeting to Decide Who Should Manage the Bison Range," *Char-Koosta News*, 34 (No. 29, May 8, 2003), 1.

56. Jennifer Greene, "Bison Range Forum Draws Large Crowd," *Char-Koosta News*, 34 (No. 34, June 12, 2003), 1.

57. "Outside Agency to Investigate Bison Range," *Great Falls Tribune*, Oct. 19, 2006, M3.

58. Matt Gouras, "Tribe Seeks Full Management of Bison Range," *Great Falls Tribune*, Nov. 22, 2006, M2.

59. Gwen Florio, "Tribes, Feds Bring in More Security as Tension Escalates at Bison Range: Agency Trades Barbs with Salish, Kootenai," *Great Falls Tribune*, Dec. 13, 2006, 1A, 7A.

60. Mary Clare Jalonick, "Government, Tribes Forge Agreement on Bison Range," *Great Falls Tribune*, June 18, 2008, M3.

61. Thurman Trosper interview.

62. File 1411-053, Box 3, 1956, Solicitor Edmund J. Fritz to Commissioner, March 3, 1958, both in Central Classified Files, 1943-1948, Record Group 75, National Archives, Washington, D.C.; CSKT minutes, Apr. 3, 1958, 2.

63. Noel Pichette, Thurman Trosper, Doug Allard (quote) and Mary "Dolly" Linsebigler interviews; Lopach, Brown, Clow, *Tribal Government Today*, 259; John Stromnes, "Tribal Enrollment Rules Draw Fire," *Missoulian*, March 26, 1997, B1, B3.

64. Ron Selden, "Court Ruling Leads to Power Struggle Among Tribal Officials," *Missoulian*, June 11, 1995, B4; Thurman Trosper interview.

65. Noel Pichette and Thurman Trosper (quote) interviews.

66. Noel Pichette (first quote), Mary "Dolly" Linsebigler (second quote) and Thurman Trosper interviews.

67. Augustine Mathias, Elmo, "Wake Up — They're Out to Get Our Resources," Letter to the Editor, *Char-Koosta News*, 31 (No. 2, Oct. 8, 1999), 4.

68. John Stromnes, "Issue: Tribal Membership," *Missoulian*, Jan. 8, 1997, B3.

69. John Carter, Tribal Legal Department, to Chairman Fred Matt and members of the tribal council, Oct. 17, 2000, 1-6, in author's possession. Fred Matt followed Mickey Pablo as chairman after Pablo's sudden death in February 2000. Matt was the chairman representing the St. Ignatius district until he lost his re-election bid in 2005.

70. Fred Matt, Chairman, to the concerned tribal members, Oct. 17, 2000, 1-2, in author's possession.

71. Deward E. Walker, Jr., "Population Projections for the Confederated Salish and Kootenai Tribes of the Flathead Indian Reservation: Final Report, December 16, 2002," (Walker Research Group, Ltd., Boulder, Col., 2002).

72. John Stromnes, "Court Won't Halt Tribal Election: Ruling a Blow for Flathead Indian Group Seeking to Limit Membership," *Missoulian*, Jan. 1, 2003, B1.

73. Arthur G. Barber, "Give Children Their Inheritance;" Regina Parot, "Your Vote Is Secret;" Letters to the Editor, *Char-Koosta News*, 34 (No. 12, Jan. 9, 2003), 4.

74. Jacqueline Britton, "Tribal Member's Children Have Limited Access to Health Care and Education Because They Are Not Enrolled;" Lillian Hartung, "You Won't Lose Benefits;" Letters, *Char-Koosta News*, 34 (No. 12, Jan. 9, 2003), 4 (second quote).

75. Vera Rosengren, "Enroll Descendants;" Nancy Brown Vaughan, "People of Mixed Heritage Have Been Here All Along"; Letters, *Char-Koosta New*, 34 (No. 13, Jan. 16, 2003), 5 (second quote).

76. Susan Dowdall, "Vote NO to Subjugation!;" Cainan Monroe, "Don't Destroy the Tribes;" *Char-Koosta News*, 34 (No. 13, Jan. 16, 2003), 5 (quotes).

77. D. Matt, "Vote in Secretarial Election This Saturday," *Char-Koosta News*, 34 (No. 13, Jan. 16, 2003), 1.

78. John Stromnes, "Historic Election Saturday Could Alter Tribal Enrollment," *Missoulian*, Jan. 17, 2003, B5.

79. John Stromnes, "Proposed Tribal Rules Fail at Polls: Salish, Kootenai Referendum Decides Issue of Desdendancy," *Missoulian*, Jan. 19, 2003, B1, B5.

80. John Stromnes, "Effort to Change Tribal Enrollment Abandoned: Spokesman Says Membership Rules Will Lead to Tribe's Extinction," *Missoulian*, Jan. 21, 2003, B1, B2.

81. Doug Allard interview with author, at Allard's Trading Post in St. Ignatius, June 24, 2004.

82. John Stromnes, "Chairman Makes Call for Unity," *Missoulian*, Jan. 22, 2003, B1, B2.

83. Ignace Couture interview, Kootenai Community Center, Elmo, Mont., June 23, 2004.

84. Al Hewankorn and Sadie Saloway interviews.

85. Francis Auld and Adeline Mathias interviews.

86. Lois Friedlander interview with author, Dayton, Mont., June 25, 2004.

87. CSKT minutes, Jan. 28, 2003, 1-3.

88. "Council Says Insufficient Grounds to Remove Polson District Council Member," *Char-Koosta News*, 34 (No. 18, Feb. 20, 2003), 1-2.

Conclusion

1. Laurie Arnold, *Bartering with the Bones of Their Dead: The Colville Confederated Tribes and Termination* (Seattle: University of Washington Press, 2012).

Index

About the Author

Jaakko Puisto, native of Finland, finished his BA in History at the University of Turku, Finland, and moved to the United States for graduate studies in 1993. He earned his PhD in History at Arizona State University in 2000. At ASU he studied under the guidance of Professor Peter Iverson, a preeminent scholar of Native American History. Dr. Puisto has published articles in *Montana: The Magazine of Western History* and the *American Indian Culture and Research Journal*. He has taught history at California State University, Stanislaus; history and Native American Studies at Montana State University, Northern; and currently teaches History at Scottsdale Community College in Arizona.